how2become

A Police Community Support Officer (PCSO)

The Insider's Guide

9112000278872

Orders: Please contact How2become Ltd, Suite 2, 50 Churchill Square Business Centre, Kings Hill, Kent ME19 4YU.

Telephone: (44) 0845 643 1299 - Lines are open Monday to Friday 9am until 5pm. Fax: (44) 01732 525965. You can also order via the e mail address info@how2become.co.uk.

ISBN: 978-1-910602-27-0

First published 2010

Copyright © 2015 how2become Ltd.

Typeset for How2become Ltd by Anton Pshinka.

Printed in Great Britain for How2become Ltd by: CMP (uk) Limited, Poole, Dorset.

CONTENTS

INTRODUCTION

Dear Sir/Madam,

Welcome to how2become a Police Community Support Officer: The Insider's Guide. This guide has been designed to help you prepare for and pass the PCSO selection process. You will find the guide both a comprehensive and highly informative tool for helping you obtain a highly desirable career within the public sector.

The great thing about being a PCSO is that you are 'community centred'. Effectively this means that you will spend more time out in the community than your average Police Officer does. Working within the local community has many benefits. You get to act as the eyes and ears for the Police Force, and you also get to build some very special relationships, both with your work colleagues and also with stakeholders in the community. PCSOs do not have the same powers as a regular Police Officer. However, they are a crucial part of the crime prevention process and are an integral part of the Police Force team.

If you would like any further assistance with the PCSO selection process then we offer the following products and training courses via the website www.how2become.com:

- How to pass the PCSO Role-Play DVD;

- How to pass the PCSO Interview DVD;

- PCSO online testing facility;

- 1 Day PCSO training course.

Finally, you won't achieve much in life without hard work, determination and perseverance. Work hard, stay focused and be what you want!

Good luck and best wishes,

The how2become team

The How2become team

PREFACE

By Author Richard McMunn

It's probably important that I start off by explaining a little bit about myself, my background, and also why I'm suitably qualified to help you pass the selection process for becoming a PCSO.

At the time of writing I am 44 years old and live in the small seaside town on the Kent Coast. I moved to the coast approximately seven years ago so that I could spend time in a suitable place writing career guides like this one. I've had a varied and successful career, both in the Royal Navy and the Fire Service.

I left school at the usual age with only three GCSEs to my name – English literature, English language and Art. What was I going to do with them, I asked myself! So, in order to get some life experience and start earning some money, I decided to join the Fleet Air Arm branch of the Royal Navy. That turned out to be quite a good decision as it taught me how to be self-disciplined, organised and most importantly to persevere until I achieved a task or goal. The qualities that I learnt in the Royal Navy are still with me today.

After four great years in the Royal Navy I left to join the Fire Service. As you are probably aware, the Fire Service is not very easy to join, in fact it is damn hard! However, I worked extremely hard, persevered and on the 25th of April 1989 I joined Kent Fire Brigade as a recruit Firefighter. Over the next 17 years I enjoyed a great career. At one point I was the youngest Officer in the service and I always worked very hard to pass my exams and promotions. I estimate that during my time in the service I was successful at over 95% of interviews I attended. This success rate wasn't down to luck, and it certainly wasn't down to my qualifications, it was simply down to hard work and perseverance.

The point I am making here is that you can be successful if you really want something. If you want to pass the selection process and become a PCSO then trust me, you can do it!

The way to pass the selection process is to embark on a comprehensive period of intense preparation. I would urge you to use an action plan during your preparation. This will allow you to focus your mind on exactly what you need to do in order to pass. I use action plans in just about every element of my work. Action plans work simply because they focus your mind on what needs to be done. Once you have created your action plan, stick it in a prominent position such as your fridge door. This will act as a reminder of the work that you need to do in order to prepare properly for selection. Your action plan might look something like this:

My weekly action plan for preparing for PCSO selection

Monday	Tuesday	Wednesday	Thursday	Friday
Learn about the role of a PCSO including reading the job description.	60 minutes study reading and learning the PCSO core competencies.	Learn how to create an effective report and try out two sample exercises.	Prepare my responses to the interview questions and try out a mock interview.	Dedicate time to completing my application, making sure I cover the core competencies.
60 minutes reading the application form, guidance notes and accompanying literature.	30 minutes learning and understanding the PCSO selection process, in particular the assessment centre.	30 minutes reading the PCSO core competencies.	60 minutes role-play practice with a friend or relative, concentrating on the assessable core competencies.	60 minutes trying out a number of sample role-play scenarios with a friend or relative.

30-minute jog or brisk walk.	30 minutes gym work.	20 minutes reading about the role of a PCSO and studying the Force's website.	30 minutes light gym work and bleep test preparation.	20-minute jog or brisk walk.

Note: Saturday and Sunday, rest days.

The above sample action plan is just a simple example of what you may wish to include. The content of your action plan will very much depend on your strengths and weaknesses. After reading this guide, decide which areas you need to work on and then add them to your action plan. Areas that you may wish to include in your action plan could be:

- Researching the role of a PCSO and studying the Police Force's website;

- Carrying out preparation for the report writing assessments;

- Improving my fitness including trying out the bleep test;

- Learning the core competencies that are relevant to the role of a PCSO;

- Carrying out a number of role-play scenarios with a friend or relative;

- Reading the recruitment literature and application form guidance notes;

- Preparing for the interview questions;

- Trying out a mock interview with a friend or relative.

The aim of this guide is to teach you the importance of preparation. As previously mentioned, during my career I have been successful at over 95% of interviews and assessments that I have attended. The reason for this is simply because I always embark on a period of focused preparation, and I always aim to improve on my weak areas. I would always carry out a mock interview before I attended the real thing. This would allow me to have a go at responding to the possible interview questions I might be asked during the real thing. This in itself allowed me to improve my confidence greatly. Follow this simple process and you too can enjoy the same levels of success that I have enjoyed.

Finally, it is very important that you believe in your own abilities. It does not matter if you have no qualifications. It does not matter if you have no knowledge yet of the role of a PCSO, the work they carry out, or the all-important core competencies. What does matter is self-belief, self-discipline and a genuine desire to improve and become successful.

Enjoy reading the guide and then set out on a period of intense preparation!

Best wishes,

Richard McMunn

Richard McMunn

Every effort has been made to ensure that the information contained within this guide is accurate at the time of publication. How2become Ltd is not responsible for anyone failing any part of the Police Community Support Officer selection process as a result of the information contained within this guide. How2become Ltd and their authors cannot accept any responsibility for any errors or omissions within this guide, however caused. No responsibility for loss or damage occasioned by any person acting, or refraining from action, as a result of the material in this publication can be accepted by How2become Ltd.

The information within this guide does not represent the views of the Police Force or any other third party organisation.

CHAPTER 1

THE ROLE
OF A PCSO

Police Community Support Officers (PCSOs) do a fantastic job in the community. Whilst opinion on their effectiveness has sometimes been divided, there is no doubting the requirement for a more visible presence from the police on our streets, and PCSOs serve that purpose very well. The emphasis for the UK Police Force is to 'engage' with local communities. This cannot be achieved by police officers alone, and therefore PCSOs play a pivotal role in acting as the link between communities and the force itself.

PCSOs are uniformed staff whose role is primarily to support the work of police officers. They assist the police in areas that need a certain level of police presence, but not necessarily the expertise of a trained police officer. An example of this would be in a predominantly rural location where crime is low, yet a presence is still required for situations such as anti-social behaviour and minor occurrences of criminal damage. Prior to the introduction of PCSOs, this kind of work would be the responsibility of the police officer. Whilst police officers will still become involved in these types of incidents when required, they are now free to carry out more effective tasks in line with their expertise and role.

PCSOs are more commonly involved in work such as:

- Providing a visible and reassuring presence within communities;
- Attending incidents of disorder, nuisance and antisocial behaviour;
- Dealing with community issues such as littering and dog fouling;
- Checking out abandoned vehicles;
- Gathering evidence through observation;
- Helping with missing persons enquiries;

- Speaking to young people who might be drunk and causing problems;
- Confiscating alcohol and tobacco;
- Crowd control and directing traffic at public events;
- Helping direct traffic at roadblocks or scenes of accidents;
- Assisting police with recording names and addresses or door-to-door enquiries.

PCSOs spend most of their time out on patrol, which is good news! Many jobs in the public sector require you to sit behind a desk in front of a computer for hours on end. Having had plenty of experience in a role of this nature, I can tell you it doesn't come recommended!

Having the freedom and the ability to patrol on foot, or possibly also on a bicycle, is one of the major attractions of the role. You will usually work in pairs and you will get to meet many different people from the community in which you live. At all times you will have access to a dedicated police officer or sergeant who can provide you with support and guidance as and when required.

PCSOs do not have the same powers of arrest as police officers, although they do have the right to detain suspected offenders for up to thirty minutes until a police officer arrives. They carry radios so that they can communicate with police control rooms and other colleagues.

WHAT DOES IT TAKE TO BECOME A PCSO?

- A confident, level-headed, positive and mature manner;
- Experience and willingness in dealing with difficult people and situations;

- To be sensitive, but thick-skinned;

- Good communication skills with regard to working with police officers;

- Good team-working skills;

- Stamina for long periods of foot patrol and shift work;

- Good communication skills to deal with all types of people, some of whom may be drunk, hostile or upset;

- Accuracy when completing paperwork;

- An appreciation of the confidential nature of police work.

WORKING HOURS AND CONDITIONS

PCSOs usually work 37 hours a week, in a shift system, covering the hours between 8am and midnight, including weekends and public holidays. There are opportunities to work part-time and flexible hours.

PCSOs are often based at local police stations in the Community Safety department, but they spend the majority of their time out on patrol, usually on foot. They may be outside in all weathers. They are often sent out to patrol areas experiencing particular problems, such as estates where there has been a spate of car thefts or burglaries, or communities where there have been complaints about nuisance youths on the streets. They wear a high-visibility uniform, which is similar to a police uniform, and includes a hat. They may wear a protective vest, but do not carry items such as handcuffs or batons.

SALARY AND BENEFITS

PCSOs enjoy a very reasonable salary and good benefits. These figures are only a guide, as actual rates of pay may vary, depending on the employer and where people live.

- A newly recruited PCSO earns about £18,000 a year (please check with your local force for exact pay rates).
- At the top of the scale they earn approximately £27,000 a year.
- Overtime and shift allowances may be available, although this varies between forces.
- Up to 25 days paid holiday per year.

NOTE Please check with your local force for exact pay scales and benefits as these do vary. You can also find out more about the role and the benefits at the website www.policecouldyou.co.uk.

THE QUALITIES OF A PCSO

The qualities of a PCSO are assessed throughout the duration of the selection process. If you are to have any chance of success then I urge you to learn these and match them at every stage. The qualities themselves are more commonly referred to as the 'core competencies'.

Effective Communication
As a PCSO you will need to communicate with different members of the community. In addition to this you will also need to communicate effectively with your work colleagues and officers, both verbally and in written format.

Community and Customer Focus
As previously stated, you will work within your local community, speaking to members of the public, gathering

evidence and building relationships. An ability to focus on the customer (member of the public) is crucial to the role. You will be assessed against this important quality during the selection process.

Problem Solving
PCSOs are required to solve many different and varied problems. For example, you may be required to investigate an alleged incident of antisocial behaviour on an estate, which requires you to gather information and make sound decisions. Part of the problem-solving process involves assessing the risks and taking appropriate courses of action that are applicable to each individual problem. As a PCSO you cannot shirk responsibility. People will expect you to make decisions based on sound judgement.

Respect for Race and Diversity
The quality of respect for race and diversity is assessed heavily during the PCSO selection process. You must be capable of understanding other people's views and be able to take them into account at all times. This means sometimes challenging your own views and beliefs in order to see things from other people's point of view. Treating people fairly is crucial to the role. Both within the workplace and out in the community you will meet people who are different from you in terms of age, background, sexual orientation, gender, disability and religious beliefs. You must treat people with dignity and respect at all times. No form of bullying or harassment is ever accepted within the Police Force.

Team Working
The Police Force is an exceptional team-working unit. They have to be in order to tackle their everyday duties. Being an effective team member is not as easy as it may first seem. During my time both in the Fire Service and the Royal Navy

you had to be effective at team working. In fact, the Fire Service placed so much emphasis on effective team working that we would hold regular meetings and briefings to assess our performance as a team.

If you cannot work with others as part of a wider team then you will not succeed as a PCSO.

Personal Responsibility

Personal responsibility is all about being self-disciplined, committed, motivated, organised and conscientious. When you arrive at incidents as a PCSO, members of the public will expect you take control and resolve the situation. They do not care that you don't have as many powers as a police officer. They will see a person in uniform and expect them to deliver. You will need to take personal responsibility during everyday situations and make sound decisions based on the information you are provided with.

So, there you have it, the personal qualities that are required to become a competent PCSO. As previously stated, these qualities are often referred to as 'core competencies'. You will be assessed against the core competencies during every stage of the selection process. My advice is that you obtain a copy of the core competencies and keep them with you when preparing for every stage of the selection process.

Resilience

Part of showing Resilience is being able to operate and make decisions in difficult and challenging situations. You will need to be able to control your emotions, remain calm and cope with certain levels of stress caused by many of the situations you will have to deal with on a daily basis. You will also need to show a level of confidence to perform your role the majority of the time without any support.

THE PCSO SELECTION PROCESS

How and Where to Apply

Before I venture into the actual PCSO selection process, let us take a look at how and when you can apply.

To begin with you need to see whether your chosen Police Force is recruiting PCSOs. This can be done by visiting the force's website or by contacting them by telephone or email. PCSO recruitment is usually carried out centrally although the UK Police Force does have a tendency to change their procedures. The most useful website for up-to-date recruitment information and contact details is as follows: www.policecouldyou.co.uk

Once you have established that your chosen force is recruiting, you need to obtain an application form. This can be done by visiting the website of the force you wish to apply for.

The PCSO selection process consists of the following format:

THE APPLICATION FORM

THE ASSESSMENT CENTRE

FITNESS TEST (Limited Forces only)

MEDICAL, SECURITY AND REFERENCES

THE APPLICATION FORM

The application form is the first stage of the selection process. Here the force will assess to see whether or not you meet the minimum eligibility requirements for the role, and also how you match the core competencies. The contents of application forms can vary from force to force. The reason for this is that the PCSO job description can vary depending on the requirements of each Police Force.

The form usually consists of five different sections as follows:

1. About you
2. About your employment
3. About your education and skills
4. Competency Assessment
5. Declaration

Providing that you follow the guidance notes that are contained within the form, the majority of the sections are relatively easy to complete. Read the form at least twice before completing it and look for important instructions such as 'Complete in Black Ink' or specific word limits when responding to the competency assessment questions.

Within a later section of the guide I will provide you with some crucial tips on how to complete the form accurately.

THE ASSESSMENT CENTRE

If your application is successful the Police will invite you to their regional Assessment Centre so that you can undertake the selection process. This involves a written test, an interview and two interactive role-plays.

Your performance will be measured against the set of skills identified as necessary for the role of PCSO, including the core competencies.

See the Assessment Centre section of this guide for more details on how to prepare for, and pass this stage of the process.

MEDICAL, SECURITY AND REFERENCES

If you successfully pass the Assessment Centre, then you will be recommended for appointment subject to satisfactory checks on your security status, medical and fitness, and references. Please note that some Police Forces require you to pass a fitness test, details of which now follow.

THE FITNESS TEST

The Endurance Test

The endurance test, also known as the 'multi-stage fitness test', 'bleep' or 'shuttle run' test, is often used by sports coaches and trainers to estimate an athlete's VO2 Max (maximum oxygen uptake). Apart from the Police, the test is also used by the Armed Forces, Emergency Services and Prison Service as part of their selection process but it is also a great way to improve and monitor your own fitness level.

Description

The 'bleep' test involves running continuously between two points that are 15 metres apart. These 'shuttle' runs are done in time to pre-recorded 'bleep' sounds on an audio CD or cassette. The time between the recorded 'bleeps' decreases after each minute and therefore the test becomes progressively harder with each level completed. The full test consists of approximately 23 levels but the actual PCSO endurance test only requires you to achieve 4 shuttles at level 5 to pass. Each level lasts approximately 60 seconds.

A level is basically a series of 15 metre 'shuttle runs'. The starting speed is normally 8.5 km/hr and then increases by 0.5km/hr with each new level.

To purchase the PCSO endurance test visit:
www.how2become.com

The Dynamic Strength Test

This test mimics a seated bench press action and a seated rowing action. You will be asked to perform 5 repetitions on both the push and pull aspects. The machine works out the average of your 5 repetitions and gives you a score.

You must Push 34 kg and Pull 35 kg to pass.

One of the most effective ways to prepare for this type of test is both by rowing (using a rowing machine) and carrying out bench press exercises. The reason why we recommend rowing during your preparation is that, apart from increasing your physical strength, it will also help prepare you for the endurance test.

Within the 'How to get PCSO fit' section of your guide I have provided you with some useful tips and exercises.

IMPORTANT Make sure you consult a medical practitioner prior to engaging in any strenuous physical exercise program.

Swimming Assessment

Police Community Support Officers may be first on the scene at emergency situations, many of which involve water. Depending on the force that you are applying to join, you may be required to take a swimming assessment. The swimming assessment enables the force to identify if your swimming ability is adequate.

Please contact your local Police Force to establish whether you are required to take a swimming assessment.

During the next section of the guide I will provide you with 10 invaluable tips that will help you prepare effectively for the PCSO selection process. Whilst some of the tips appear to be obvious, it is these that most applicants fail to concentrate on and as a result they end up failing. Follow each tip carefully and implement them into your preparation strategy.

CHAPTER 2

THE TOP TEN
INSIDER TIPS
AND ADVICE

TIP 1
Be fully prepared and fully focused

This is your opportunity to get yourself a well-paid, well-respected and secure career in the Police Force. Therefore, it is worth putting in the extra effort during your preparation.

When you are applying for any career, it is of vital importance that you prepare yourself fully. What I mean is that you do everything you can to find out what is required of you. Most people do not read the guidance notes on the application form and then they wonder why they didn't get through to the next stage. Make sure you read every bit of information you receive at least twice and understand what is required. Things in life do not come easy and you must be prepared to work hard.

Whenever you come up against hurdles or difficult situations and experiences, always try to look for the opportunity to improve yourself. For example, if you have applied to become a PCSO before, what have you done to improve your chances of success the second time around? Did you find out what areas you failed on, and if so, have you done anything about it?

During the beginning of this guide I made reference to an action plan. I strongly urge you to use an action plan during selection. Put yourself out and make the effort to work on your weak areas. Make sure you set aside plenty of time to complete the application form. Make sure you work on your written communication skills and make sure you carry out mock interviews and role-play scenarios. Coupled with all of this, you should carry out a structured training programme during your preparation – regardless of whether or not you have to go through a fitness test. By keeping fit, your motivation levels will increase and so too will your ability to concentrate.

TIP 2
Understand equality and fairness and respect diversity at all times

Equality and fairness are crucial in today's society. We must treat each other with respect and dignity, and understand that people come from different backgrounds and cultures to ourselves. As we all know, the community in which we live is diverse in nature, and so should the Police Force be if it is to be capable of delivering the high quality service that the public expects.

Treat people how you expect to be treated – with dignity and respect. If you do not believe in equality, fairness and dignity then you are applying for the wrong job. PCSOs are role models and people will look to you to set an example in society. Part of the application process will test your understanding, knowledge and application of equality and fairness issues in the application form, interview and role-play scenarios. There are many ways in which you can prepare for these to help improve your knowledge and understanding of this important topic. Within this guide I have provided you with useful tips and advice and I recommend you spend time reading the equality and fairness section of the guide.

Don't leave it to chance! Make sure you understand exactly what equality and fairness means and what it stands for.

TIP 3
Understand the core competencies

The PCSO core competencies form the fundamental requirements of your role. They identify how you should perform and are key to your role as a Police Community Support Officer. Read them and make sure you understand them. They are key to your success! Just like a house is built on solid foundations, the core competencies are the foundations of the role of a PCSO. If they are in place, then a PCSO will perform to a high standard.

Throughout the application process, you should concentrate on the core competencies, constantly trying to demonstrate them at every stage.

When completing the application form your answers should be based around the core competencies. The same rule applies to the interview and role-play exercises. Whenever you prepare a response you need to structure it around the core competencies. These are the first thing you should learn. Learn the core competencies and you will find that the remainder of your preparation will be far easier.

The core competencies cover a wide range of required skills and attributes including team work, customer focus, problem-solving and equality and fairness issues to name but a few.

This is the most important tip I can provide you with – Don't ignore it!

TIP 4
Use keywords and phrases from the core competencies during your application form responses
The majority of people who apply to become PCSOs will complete their application form without making an effort to match the core competencies. The person who has the task of assessing your form is looking to see how closely you match the assessable core competencies. In order to achieve this you should use keywords and phrases from the core competencies in your responses to the competency assessment.

Here's an example of how you can match the core competency of Respect for Race and Diversity. Part of the core competency states:

Understands other people's views and takes them into account. Is tactful and diplomatic when dealing with people, treating them with dignity and respect at all times. Understands and is sensitive to social, cultural and racial differences.

When constructing my response to a question that assesses this core competency I will use keywords and phrases from the content in order to improve my chances of success:

'When dealing with the man I made sure that I listened carefully to his views, taking onboard his comments. I was respectful towards him at all times and took into account our differences, which in turn helped me to deal with him in a sensitive manner.'

You will see from the above statement that I have incorporated keywords from the core competency. Not only does this make the assessor's life a lot easier, it also ensures that you match the core competencies, something that is crucial to your success.

You can use this tip not only on the application form, but also during the report writing, role-play scenarios and the interview. It works to great effect!

TIP 5
During the role play scenarios concentrate on delivering high quality customer service

Having personally been through the PCSO selection process myself, I can safely say that the role-play scenarios are probably the hardest part of the assessment centre. Many people find the role-plays a daunting process, which is why you should practise them prior to attending the assessment centre.

The purpose of the role-play scenarios is to assess how you interact with people during certain scenarios that are similar to the type you will encounter as a PCSO. If you can deal with these scenarios effectively, then you are more than likely going to be able to deal with them in real life as a PCSO.

Although 'customer focus' is only one of the role-play assessable areas, it is one that I urge you to demonstrate at all times. Customer focus essentially means concentrating on the customer, dealing with them in a sensitive manner, and making sure you listen to their needs and requirements. It will be your job to listen to the role-play actor during each scenario carefully, ask them relevant questions, and provide a suitable solution to the problem.

Remember that the Police Force is committed to delivering a high quality service. Focus on demonstrating this during the role-play scenarios and you will increase your chances of success.

TIP 6
Learn the welcome pack before you go to the selection centre
Prior to the selection centre you will be sent a welcome pack. Within the pack you will find details relating to the role you are required to undertake as part of the assessment. That role will normally be as a customer service manager at a fictitious retail centre called the Westshire Centre. It is my strong belief that those candidates who read and absorb the welcome pack prior to their day have a greater chance of succeeding.

The role-play assessment is divided into two parts as follows:

• The preparation phase

• The activity phase

The two phases basically speak for themselves. The preparation phase is where you get yourself ready for the activity phase. This involves 5 minutes reading the welcome pack and also studying the scenario that you will undertake during the activity stage. The vast majority of candidates who attend the selection centre will not read the welcome pack or guidance notes until they sit down at the preparation phase. This is a huge mistake!

If you learn your role and responsibilities prior to the selection centre then you are halfway there. This will then give you plenty of time to prepare for the scenario, take notes and prepare yourself mentally. Remember that preparation is the all-important word!

TIP 7
Be prepared to challenge inappropriate behaviour

The core competency of Respect for Race and Diversity is assessed heavily during the selection process. In fact, if you score a D at any point in this area you will automatically fail the entire selection! Therefore, it is worth taking note of the following advice.

First of all, why do the Police place so much emphasis on this important competency? The answer is, because we live in a society that is diverse in nature. With that in mind, you will be dealing with people from all walks of life. Any form of bullying, racism or harassment is totally unacceptable, not only in the Police Force, but also in society as a whole. You need to be prepared to challenge, in an appropriate manner, any behaviour that is bullying, discriminatory or inappropriate.

You will be assessed against this important area throughout the selection process. In particular you may find that one of the role-play scenarios requires you to challenge the role actor due to their comments or actions. If you fail to challenge the inappropriate behaviour in the correct manner then you could fail the entire selection.

TIP 8
Don't stop until you achieve your goal
If you don't reach the required standard at the first or subsequent attempts, don't give up. So long as you always try to better yourself, there is always the chance that you will succeed. If you do fail any of the stages look at the area(s) you need to improve on.

Did you fail the application form? If so then there are ways of improving. Don't just sit back and wait for the next opportunity to come along, prepare for it straight away and you'll increase your chances for next time.

Many people give up on their goals far too easily. Learning to find the positive aspects of negative situations is a difficult thing to do but a skill that anyone can acquire through practice and determination. If you really want to achieve your goals then anything is possible.

During your preparation set yourself small targets each week. For example, your first week may be used to concentrate on learning the core competencies that are relevant to a PCSO. Your second week can be used to prepare for your written responses on the application form, and so on. If you get tired or feel de-motivated at any time during your preparation, walk away from it and give yourself a break. You may find that you come back to it re-energised, more focused and determined to succeed!

TIP 9
Practise the role-play exercises with a friend or relative
The role-play scenarios can be a daunting experience, especially if you've never done anything like this before.

Whilst the Police Force will advise you to be yourself, there are ways in which you can prepare and subsequently increase your chances of success.

The way to prepare for the role-plays is to act them out in a room with a friend or relative. Within this guide you have been provided with a number of example role-play scenarios. Use these to practise with, and hone your skills in each area of the core competencies that are being assessed.

The only way that you will be able to understand what is required during the role-play exercises is to learn the assessable core competencies. For example, if you are being assessed against the core competency of customer focus, then you will need to demonstrate the following during each role-play scenario:

• Be professional and present an appropriate image in line with your brief and job description.

• Focus on the needs of the customer in every scenario.

• Sort out any problems as soon as possible and apologise for any errors or mistakes that have been made.

• Ask the customer whether they are satisfied with your actions or not. If they are not, then take alternative steps to make them satisfied if possible.

• Keep the customer updated on progress.

Doing all of the above, in addition to covering the other assessable areas, can be quite a difficult task. However, if you practise these skills regularly in the build up to your assessment then you will find it becomes easier and easier the more that you do.

TIP 10
Practise a mock interview

Mock interviews are a fantastic way to prepare for both the assessment centre and interview. They not only allow you to practise your responses to the questions, but they are fantastic for improving your confidence and overall ability.

During the build up to interviews in the past, I would write down a number of predicted interview questions that I had created during my research. I would then ask a friend or relative to ask me these questions under formal interview conditions. I found this to be excellent preparation and it certainly served me well during all of my career interviews. I would estimate that I was successful at over 95% of all interviews I attended. I put this success purely down to this form of preparation.

I would also strongly recommend that you sit down in front of a long mirror and respond to the same set of interview questions. Watch your interview technique. Do you slouch? Do you fidget and do you overuse your hands?

It is important that you work on your interview technique during the build up to the assessment centre and the final interview.

Do not make the mistake of carrying out little or no preparation, because you can be guaranteed that some of the other candidates will have prepared fully. Make sure you put in the time and effort and practise a number of mock interviews. You will be amazed at how confident you feel during the real interview.

CHAPTER 3

COMPLETING
THE APPLICATION
FORM

INTRODUCTION

PCSO application forms vary from force to force. Regardless of the application form questions or format, there are a few fundamental principles that you need to follow whilst completing the form and these will be covered within this section of the guide.

It is important that you set aside plenty of time to complete the form correctly in order to give yourself every opportunity of success. In order to assist you in the completion of your application form I have provided you with a step-by-step guide. Please read each of the following tips very carefully.

TIP 1
Before you complete the application form, read it thoroughly and at least twice
Make sure you focus on the guidance notes in particular. This is important, as there are normally some important instructions to follow. For example, some forms request that you complete them in 'black ink'. If you complete them in blue or a different colour, then your submission will be rejected.

Being able to follow simple instructions is fundamental to the role of a PCSO.

TIP 2
Read the job description/person specification prior to completing the form
This is very important, as you will be assessed on your ability to match this during each stage of the selection process. The job description/person specification is sometimes split into two areas, these being the 'essential' criteria and the 'desirable' criteria.

Obviously, you must ensure that you meet the 'essential' criteria at each stage of the process in order to demonstrate that you have the potential to perform the PCSO role. The 'desirable' criteria do not necessarily have to be met, however, the more 'desirable' criteria you can meet the higher your chances of success will be.

Before I move on to tip 3, let us take a look at an example of the 'essential criteria' that are used to assess a PCSO application form.

Essential Knowledge and Experience - Experience of working effectively as part of a team.

In this particular example, the above 'essential' criterion forms part of the application form assessment. Therefore, when completing the form you will be asked a question that allows you to demonstrate your ability to meet this criterion. An example question that could be used to assess the above criterion is as follows:

A key part of Police Community Support Officers' work involves recognising the benefits and importance of working in teams to achieve goals. Tell us about an occasion where you were working as part of a team in order to achieve a collective goal.

When responding to this question it is vitally important that you provide a suitable example of when you have worked as part of a team in order to achieve a collective goal. Do not make the mistake of telling them how you *would* work in a team, but instead provide an example of where you *have* worked as part of a team and what your role was within that team.

The key to completing the application form correctly is to make sure that you meet the assessment criteria. Many people do not read the job description/person specification and, therefore, run the risk of failing this important stage.

TIP 3
Use relevant examples when answering the questions

The PCSO Application Form will pose a number of questions that are designed to assess your ability to meet the person specification. Before responding to each question read it thoroughly first. What is the question asking you to do? Take a look at the following sub-question:

Tell us exactly what you did to try to sort out their problem, and why you did it.

The above question is asking for two things:

• *What* you did

• *Why* you did it.

Therefore, your response should be relevant to both parts of the question.

Here is an example of how this question might be answered. The 'what' part of the question is in the first sentence and the 'why' part of the question in the second.

'Immediately I tried to defuse his anger by telling him that I fully understood his situation and that I would feel exactly the same if I was in his position. I promised him that I would resolve the situation and offered him a cup of tea or coffee whilst he waited for me to address the problem. I took this action because I feel that it is important to deliver a high level of customer service in my role. I enjoy making customers happy and resolving their problems.'

TIP 4

When answering the questions make sure you write neatly, using the correct grammar, and that you keep within the allocated 'word count'

Most of the PCSO person specifications will require you to have the ability to produce accurate written information and demonstrate a high level of attention to detail.

Therefore, it is important that your application form is completed accurately and in a professional manner. Try photocopying the form before you complete it and fill in a 'rough' copy first to allow for any mistakes. Many of the questions will ask for a maximum number of words. Do not go over the allocated number of words as this may affect the scoring.

The best way to check for the correct number of words is to use the 'Word Count' tool in Microsoft Word on your computer. Open up Microsoft Word and type in your response. Then go to Tools/Word Count and this will tell you how many words are in your response.

This is a fast and effective way of ensuring that you stick to the allocated word count.

TIP 5

Match the core competencies

The PCSO core competencies form the basis of the role and they also form the basis of the assessment criteria. This means that throughout the selection process you will be assessed against these continuously. The core competencies will vary slightly from force to force. When completing the application form I suggest that you keep a copy of the core competencies next to you so that you can constantly refer to them when responding to the questions.

On the following pages I have provided you with a number of sample responses to the more common PCSO application form questions. I have provided you with a brief explanation to each question before providing a sample response. Please note that the sample responses are for demonstration purposes only. It is important that your responses are relevant to you and your own skills, knowledge and experience.

SAMPLE APPLICATION FORM QUESTION RESPONSES

Question 1

It is very important that Police Community Support Officers deliver an excellent service and actively develop good working relationships with members of the public.

Please tell us of an occasion when you had to deal with someone who was not satisfied with the way they had been treated. If possible, give an example that extends over a period of time and where your involvement went beyond just giving advice.

i) Describe the situation clearly and the reason why you think they were not satisfied.
This is a question with four parts. When answering this question, do not make the mistake of telling them how you *would* deal with such a situation, but instead explain how you *have* dealt with this type of situation in the past.

Try to include a situation where you had to contact the person more than just once, maybe to reassure them and check that they were now satisfied. A good response to this type of question would be describing where you have dealt with someone's complaint and gone out of your way to make the situation right for them. This part of the question asks you to describe the situation clearly before stating why you think they were not satisfied. Take a look at the sample response.

Sample response to Question 1, part i

'Whilst working as a sales person, I was approached by a dissatisfied customer. He explained to me that he had recently purchased a pair of trainers for his daughter. When she tried them on she noticed that one was a size 6 and the other a size 7.

Understandably he was not happy with the service he had received. The reason for his dissatisfaction was that his daughter had been let down and as a consequence he then had to travel back into town to sort out a problem that should not have occurred in the first place. The problem was caused by poor customer service and it was important that I resolved the issue for him.'

ii) What exactly did you do in response, and why?

During this part of the question you are asked to explain what you did and the reasons why you took this course of action. Remember that part of the PCSO role is to deliver excellent service and also to develop good working relationships with members of the public, therefore your response should reflect your ability to do this. Take a look at the sample response.

Sample response to Question 1, part ii

'Immediately, I tried to defuse his anger by telling him that I fully understood his situation and that I would feel exactly the same if I was in his position. I promised him that I would resolve the situation and offered him a cup of tea or coffee while he waited for me to address the issue. I took this action *because I feel that it is important to deliver a high level of customer service in my role. I would not have been happy if I had been in the same situation so I was keen to put it right for him. I enjoy making customers happy and resolving their problems.'*

iii) How did you know that the person was satisfied with your response?

This part of the question is designed to see whether you successfully resolved the issue to the satisfaction of the person(s) concerned. When someone is satisfied with the way a complaint or issue has been dealt with, they will normally express both visual and verbal signs of satisfaction. They may smile, appear to be happy, tell you that they are satisfied or even thank you for the way that you have dealt with the problem.

When responding to this question, try to include both visual and verbal indicators that the person was satisfied. Take a look at the following sample response.

Sample response to Question 1, part iii

'I could detect a change in his behaviour as soon as I explained that I sympathised with his situation. The tone in his voice became less agitated and he was now smiling so I took advantage of this situation and tried even harder to turn his bad experience with us into a positive one. When I offered him a refund, along with the replacement of the running shoes, his attitude changed again, but this time he appeared to be very satisfied. He then informed me that he would continue to shop with us despite the initial experience and thanked me for the way that I had dealt with his complaint.'

iv) What if you hadn't acted as you did? What do you think the likely outcome would have been?

This part of the question is designed to see if you have the ability to understand how important excellent customer service is. If PCSOs deliver poor customer service then this is detrimental to the Police Force and does nothing but deteriorate public relations. As a PCSO, you will need to understand why it is important to deliver an excellent service and this part of the question assesses your understanding of this. Now take a look at the sample response provided.

'To begin with, I believe the situation would have become even more heated and possibly untenable. His anger or dissatisfaction could have escalated if my attempts to de-fuse the situation had not taken place. I also believe that we would have lost a good customer and, therefore, lost future profits and custom for the company. There would have been a high possibility that the gentleman would have taken his complaint higher, either to our head office, trading standards or the local newspaper. Customer service is important and we need to do everything we can (within reason) to make the level of service we provide as high as possible.'

Question 2

It is highly important that Police Community Support Officers respect the lifestyle, culture and beliefs of others, even if these differ significantly from their own.

Please give us an example of an occasion where you have demonstrated respect for someone with a belief or lifestyle that significantly differed from your own. This may be a religious, cultural, ethical or moral belief, or some important aspect of their lifestyle.

i) Describe the situation and how you and the other person differed.

This type of question assesses your ability to work with people from all backgrounds and, in this particular instance, there are two parts to the question. Remember to answer the question based not on how you would act in this type of situation but, instead, on how you have acted. Before creating a response to this question, I recommend that you visit the 'Equality and Diversity' section of this guide. Now take a look at the following sample response.

Sample response to Question 2, part i

'Whilst working as a sales assistant at a local supermarket, I was approached by a work colleague who was from a different background. He told me that he needed to pray whilst he was at work and he asked me if I would mind covering for him on the checkout whilst he did this. I agreed to do this for him and every time he wanted to go off and pray I would stand in for him on the checkout. We differed in terms of our religious backgrounds and beliefs and, whilst I fully respect religion, I do not pray at all, whereas this was an integral part of his life.'

ii) How did you adapt your behaviour to interact with the other person and show you understood how they may have felt?

During this part of the question try to demonstrate how you went out of your way to help them. It is important that you show the assessor that you are capable of supporting the person and being sensitive to their needs where appropriate.

Sample response to Question 2, part ii

'I adapted my behaviour by making myself available for him whenever he needed me. I told him that I would cover for him at any time and that it was not a problem at all. I wanted to make him feel at ease about the situation, as he appeared to be slightly apprehensive about asking me. I assured him that

it was no problem at all and that I understood how important it was for him to pray during the day. I adapted my behaviour by making sure I was available whenever he wanted to pray. I also gave him my mobile phone number and told him to text or call me if he couldn't find me in the supermarket. That way he knew that he could get hold of me if he needed to.'

Question 3

It is vital that Police Community Support Officers act responsibly and to a high standard within their role, regardless of their perception of the importance of the task.

Tell us about an occasion when you were asked to carry out a repetitive or very basic task.

i) What was the situation and why did the task need to be carried out?

There are three parts to this particular question and they are designed to see if you have had any experience of carrying out repetitive or basic tasks. Many people become bored or agitated when carrying out mundane or tedious tasks. The role of the PCSO will sometimes involve repetitive work and the Police want to know that you have the ability to perform these tasks to a high standard, as and when required. When responding to the questions try to come across in a positive manner and provide a suitable example of where you successfully carried out and completed such a task. Now take a look at the following sample response.

Sample response to Question 3, part i

'Whilst working in my previous job as an administrative clerk for a production company, I was asked to send out 5,000 leaflets to different clients and customers. The task

involved folding the leaflets, placing them in the envelopes and attaching stamps. The task was extremely repetitive and time-consuming. In total it took me 2 weeks solid work to complete the 5,000 requested. The task needed to be carried out so that the company could promote a new product that it was selling. This was a cost effective way of promoting the product.'

ii) How did you stay focused on the task?

When responding to this question, make sure you provide evidence of your organisational and motivational skills. Try to demonstrate an understanding of the 'bigger picture' and that mundane tasks are just as important as the interesting ones when it comes to delivering a high quality service to the public. '

Sample response to Question 3, part ii

'I broke down the task into manageable portions. I ensured that I completed at least 500 every day of the week and took small five-minute breaks every half hour. By the end of the two weeks I would have completed the allocated 5,000. I realised the importance of the task and that it was essential for the business to promote its product. The company employ me and, in order for me to remain in employment with them, they need to sell their products and generate revenue. I am a highly self-motivated person and I do not mind repetitive tasks.'

iii) How did you ensure the task reached a satisfactory conclusion?

As a PCSO you will be trusted to work on your own and check that each task you carry out is done correctly. The most effective way to do this is to approach the task in an organised and methodical manner, checking everything that you do. When responding to this type of question, demonstrate a level of self-discipline and a keen eye for detail.

Sample response to Question 3, part iii

'I carried out the task methodically and in an organised manner. I maintained a list of addresses and crossed them off as each envelope was posted. This way I was able to keep a record of the ones I had completed and the ones that I still had to send off. Once I had completed the task, I randomly selected one customer from every fifty. I telephoned each one to check whether they had received the leaflet or not, and this allowed me to assess my own performance to see if I had completed the task correctly.'

Question 4

A key part of Police Community Support Officers' work involves recognising the benefits and importance of working in teams to achieve goals.

Tell us about an occasion where you worked as part of a team in order to achieve a collective goal.

i) Describe the situation and the collective goal you were aiming
to achieve.

Team work is a very important part of the PCSO's working life, as he or she will need to be able to work comfortably in a team environment. These questions are designed to assess your ability to work in this way. When responding to this question ensure you provide an actual example of where you have worked as part of a team to achieve a common goal.

Take a look at the following sample response and see how the team worked effectively to achieve the common goal of building four houses in a short space of time.

Sample response to Question 4 part i

'In my previous job I worked as a bricklayer on a local build-ing complex. I worked with four other bricklayers and three labourers. We were presented with a difficult team task that required us to work together and build four new homes in a very short space of time and under considerable pressure. The previous bricklayers had failed to complete the work to a satisfactory standard. The collective goal was to profes-sionally build the four houses in a one month period, often working around the clock to meet the deadline.'

ii) Describe your role in the team and how you worked with others.

Your role as a team player includes carrying out your job professionally and competently, communicating with other team members, and also providing support where needed. Try to include these three elements in you response.

Sample response to Question number 4, part ii

'My role in the team was to lay bricks at the gable end of each house, working alongside one of the labourers who would supply the cement and bricks. It was important that I carried out my role competently, professionally and on time. The other bricklayers built the other sides of the house and we had to work at the same pace to ensure the house was constructed evenly. We constantly communicated so that we knew what we were all doing and the progress that we had made so far. I also provided support to the other team members.'

iii) What challenges did you and the team encounter?

Every team comes up against challenges. It's what you do about those challenges that is the important factor. When responding to this question, provide evidence of how you overcame the challenges in order to complete the task.

Sample response to Question 4, part iii

'The main challenges were in relation to time and the inclement weather conditions. The company that we worked for wanted the task completed in a very short space of time so we had to work very long days, often with short breaks. We stayed motivated by talking and focusing on the end goal. We were building the houses during the winter months so the weather was not that great either but we were always focused on the task.'

iv) How did working as part of a team overcome this?

'We all stayed motivated right until the end goal was achieved. By talking to each other throughout the task and keeping everyone informed of our progress we were able to build up a strong team spirit. We all decided that one person should supply the hot soup each day whilst another person supplied the hot drinks in order to keep our energy levels up. Everybody had a role to perform and we weren't going to let each other down. By staying focused on our ultimate aim we were able to successfully achieve the task, much to the delight of the foreman.'

Question 5

It is important that anyone applying to be a Police Community Support Officer is motivated and fully understands the role.

i) What do you think you will be doing, day-to-day, as a Police Community Support Officer?

Well, there is only one way to fully understand the role of the PCSO, and that is to read about it. Your first port of call should be your recruitment literature.

Here you will find many useful facts about the PCSO role.

Try to learn the different types of jobs that a PCSO carries out, such as high-visibility, uniformed foot patrols, engaging with youths, preserving crime scenes, and interacting with schools to name but a few. Also, learn about the working hours/conditions and any information that provides an insight into a typical working day of a PCSO. You will also find some very useful contact information in the Useful Contacts section of this guide to help you research the role of the PCSO. Now take a look at the following sample response to this question.

Sample response to Question 5, part i

'As a PCSO I will be assisting the police in areas that need a certain level of police presence, but not necessarily the expertise of a trained police officer.

I will be giving a valuable service by providing a visible and reassuring presence within the community. I will attend incidents of disorder, nuisance and antisocial behaviour and, also, I will be dealing with community issues such as littering and dog fouling. Other tasks involve checking out abandoned vehicles, gathering evidence through observation, helping with missing persons enquiries and speaking to young people who might be drunk and causing problems. I would spend most of my time out on patrol, usually on foot or possibly on a bicycle.'

ii) Please explain why you would like to become a Police Community Support Officer, and what you think you can contribute.

Only you will know the reasons why you want to become a PCSO. However, if it is to chase and catch criminals then you may wish to think twice before you apply. Before you answer this question, be fully aware of the PCSO role for the force that you are applying to. You should have a keen desire to serve the community and make a difference by interacting with the members of that community. Visit the website of the force that you are applying to join (see the Useful Contacts section) and read their vision or mission statement.

The second part of this question relates to what you think you can contribute. Be positive and upbeat in your response and put yourself across in a positive manner. Take a look at the following sample response for some useful hints and tips.

Sample response to Question 5, part ii

'I would like to become a PCSO so that I can help my community. I enjoy working with people from all backgrounds and I believe that I could offer a professional and helpful service to members of the public. I believe that I would get a great deal of job satisfaction from helping others and acting as the important link between the community and the Police. I am a very good team player and always perform my tasks diligently and reliably. I understand that I would possibly have to get involved in a range of difficult situations and I am prepared for this. I have great communication skills and believe that I can talk to people in a calm and reassuring manner. I am physically fit and have the stamina for long periods of foot patrol when required. Finally, I fully appreciate the importance of the confidential nature of this work and can be relied upon to perform to a high standard at all times.'

Question 6

It is essential that PCSOs act without being told and strive to do an excellent job.

i) What was the situation and why did you feel the need to take the initiative?

ii) Exactly what did you do?

When responding to questions of this nature you must provide an example of where you have gone out of your way to do a professional and competent job. If you can demonstrate that you have gone above and beyond what is normally required then even better. Take a look at the following sample response.

Sample response to Question 6, parts i and ii

'Whilst working in my previous role as a retail sales assistant, the manager had gone out to lunch and it was during this period that the fire alarm began to sound. It was the week before Christmas and the shop was very busy. Everybody was ignoring the alarm and I decided to take the initiative and asked everybody to evacuate the shop for their own safety. The alarm has gone off in the past, but the normal manager usually lets people stay in the shop whilst he finds out if it's a false alarm. This was a difficult situation because the shop was very busy, nobody wanted to leave and the other shop assistants were disagreeing with me in my decision to evacuate the shop. Some of the customers became irate as they were in the changing rooms at the time. I decided to take the initiative because I felt that the safety of the customers was a priority.'

ii) Exactly what did you do?

'I shouted at the top of my voice that everybody was to leave the shop immediately, even though the sound of the alarm was reducing the impact of my voice. I then told one of the other assistants to dial 999 and ask for the Fire Brigade. I asked the other shop assistants to walk around the shop and tell everybody to leave whilst we investigated the problem. Eventually, after I kept persisting, everybody began to leave the shop. I went outside with the other members of staff, took a roll call, and waited for the Fire Brigade to arrive.

Question 7

Please tell us about any other skills you have such as driving or language and/or any voluntary or community activities you have been involved with, including relevant activities to support your application.

This question is relatively easy to respond to, providing that is you have the relevant skills and experiences. I believe it is important to provide evidence of community/voluntary work if possible. If you do not have any experience in this area, then why not consider arranging a charity event in your local area. You could arrange a sponsored run, swim or car wash in aid of a local good cause. Alternatively, why not dedicate one hour a week to working in a local charity shop? Being able to demonstrate experience of voluntary or community work will gain you higher scores.

Sample response to Question 7

'I have held a full clean UK driving licence for 7 years. Whilst I do not speak any additional languages, I am an excellent communicator and can respond to the needs of the community. I have regularly been involved with charity work at a local school and have helped to raise funds by organising two summer boot fairs. In total we managed to raise £1,500 for good causes in the area. I am a very fit and active person and I visit the gymnasium 3 times a week. Earlier this year, I ran the London Marathon for the first time and managed to raise £700 for a local hospital charity. Finally, I have a lot of experience of working under pressure and working as part of a team. I feel comfortable working with people from all backgrounds and believe that the skills I already possess would help me to make a competent and professional PCSO.'

FINAL TIPS FOR CREATING A STRONG APPLICATION

- Set aside plenty of time to complete the form. When I applied, I set aside five evenings of solid hard work and concentration. I read the guidance notes carefully and followed EVERY instruction. Make the effort, and you will be rewarded.

- Follow the guidance notes at all times.

- Check your spelling, grammar and punctuation. You will lose marks if you don't.

- Before you submit your form get someone to check over it for you. Don't get someone who is going to say it's good just to please you. You need constructive feedback not praise.

- If you are sending your application form by post, send it recorded delivery. I have known of many forms that have gone missing!

CHAPTER 4

EQUALITY AND DIVERSITY

> "Equality is not about treating everybody the same, but recognising we are all individuals, unique in our own way. Equality and fairness is about recognising, accepting and valuing people's unique individuality according to their needs.
>
> This often means that individuals may be treated appropriately, yet fairly, based on their needs."

Members of the community need to trust their PCSOs and be confident that they will be respected and treated fairly by them. This is particularly true of ethnic minority communities. It is of vital importance that a Police Service represents the community in which it serves. This means that a diverse community needs a diverse Police Force in order to give it the best service possible.

EQUALITY AND FAIRNESS – THE SELECTION PROCESS

During the PCSO selection process you will be assessed in the area of equality and fairness. The core competency that covers this area is Respect for Race and Diversity. I strongly advise that you obtain a copy of the core competencies and study this core competency until you understand it and are able to match it.

HOW TO MEET THIS IMPORTANT CORE COMPETENCY

During the selection process you will be required to demonstrate that you understand other people's views and take them into account. You will need to be tactful and diplomatic when dealing with people, and also demonstrate that you are capable of treating people with dignity and respect at all times, no matter what their background, status, circumstances or appearance.

Here are a number of ways in which you can match the core competency of Respect for Race and Diversity:

- You can see issues from other people's points of view;

- You are capable of treating everyone with respect and dignity;

- When dealing with people you are polite, tolerant and patient;

- Whilst sorting out arguments you are respectful of the needs of everyone involved;

- You can show understanding and also be sensitive to people's problems, vulnerabilities and needs;

- You are capable of listening to, and supporting others' needs or interests;

- You are capable of using language in an appropriate way and you are sensitive to the way it may affect others;

- Within the context of the law you can identify and respect other people's values;

- You have an ability to understand what offends other people and groups and you take this into account when dealing with them;

- You can respect confidentiality;

- You are able to deliver difficult messages honestly and sensitively;

- You are open and honest with people.

Within the application form and interview sections of this guide I have provided you with sample responses to help you match the relevant core competencies. I mention this fact on a number of occasions throughout this guide but you must read, learn, absorb and understand the core competencies relevant to each section.

During your responses to both the application form questions and the interview questions try to include some of the 'Positive Indicators' that form part of the core competencies. For example, when dealing with an incident that involves equality and fairness issues make sure you are sensitive to people's needs. Treat everyone with respect and dignity and see things from others' points of view. Try also to understand what offends people and take this into account when dealing with their problems or needs.

The core competencies are a crucial element of your success and it is important that you have a copy of them next to you when you are reading the sections that relate to the application form, the assessment centre and the interview.

TOP TIP

Visit the website of the Police Force you are applying to join and read their Race Equality Scheme (if available).

CHAPTER 5

ABOUT THE PCSO ASSESSMENT CENTRE

INTRODUCTION

Once you have successfully passed the Application Form stage of the process you will be invited to attend a Regional Assessment Centre.

The Assessment Centre's location will vary from force to force but you will be provided with details, times and location before you attend. Make sure you know exactly where your venue is and don't be late!

This Centre will provide the Police with information regarding your suitability for recruitment into the Police Service as a PCSO. The Selection Centre tests are usually conducted over a period of three to four hours and you will either attend in the morning or in the afternoon. For the Selection Centre you will be required to take a number of important documents with you to confirm your identification to the Police, including:

A full 10-year passport or TWO of the following:

- British Driving Licence;
- P45;
- Birth Certificate: issued within six weeks of birth;
- Cheque Book and Bank Card with three statements and proof of signature;
- Card containing a photograph of yourself;
- Proof of residence, e.g. Council Tax, Gas, Electricity, Water or Telephone Bill.

Make sure that you read the information given to you and take along the relevant documents as if you do not then you won't be able to continue with the day.

We strongly advise that you read the 'PCSO selection centre diaries' section in order to get a full understanding of what the day involves from an insider's perspective. Within this section of the guide I have provided you with as much information as possible to try to cover every eventuality. Please bear in mind that not all of the information will apply to you and it is important that you take the time to choose which information is applicable.

In the majority of cases the PCSO Assessment Centre tests follow a similar format as those for a regular Police Officer, with the exception that there will only be two interactive Role-Plays.

The most important thing to remember at the Assessment Centre is that you will be assessed against the Core Competencies that have been defined for your particular PCSO role. Examples of these are indicated as follows.

PCSO ASSESSABLE CORE COMPETENCIES (SAMPLE ONLY)

Effective communication
Communicates all needs, instructions and decisions clearly. Adapts the style of communication to meet the needs of the audience.

During the assessment centre you will need to demonstrate effective communication skills. This will be in written format during the report writing exercises and verbally during both the role-plays and the interview.

Community and customer focus
Sees things from the public's point of view and encourages others to do the same. Builds a good understanding and relationship within the community that is served.

As you can imagine, PCSOs are required to have a good understanding of their community. If they understand the needs of their community then they are far more likely to deliver a high standard of service. They must also be able to have the interests of their customers (the public) at the forefront of their minds. During the role-play scenarios you will be required to demonstrate your ability to provide a high level of service at all times.

Problem solving
Gathers information from a range of sources to understand situations, making sure it is reliable and accurate. Identifies risks and considers alternative courses of action to make good decisions.

In order to solve problems effectively you will need to gather information. This means asking relevant questions of the role-play actor, which in turn will enable you to make suitable decisions.

Respect for race and diversity
Understands other people's views and takes them into account. Treats people with dignity and respect at all times, no matter what their background, status, circumstances or appearance.

This core competency is very important. You must treat people with dignity and respect at all times. In addition to treating people in the right way, you will also be required to challenge any comments or behaviour that is either inappropriate or discriminatory.

Team working
Works effectively as a team member and helps build rela-tionships within it.

If you cannot work as part of a team then the job of a PCSO is not for you. It is crucial that you are able to demonstrate effective team-working skills during the assessment centre.

Personal responsibility
Takes personal responsibility for making things happen and achieving results. Displays motivation, commitment, perseverance and conscientiousness. Acts with a high degree of integrity.

Takes personal responsibility for own actions and sorts out issues or problems that arise. Is focused on achieving results to required standard and developing skills and knowledge.

It will be your job to take personal responsibility for making things happen as a PCSO. More often than not, the decisions that you will make will be whilst under pressure. During the assessment centre you must show the assessors that you can take responsibility for all matters and situations.

The core competencies/skills that you will be assessed against will be provided in your information pack, which the Police will send you in plenty of time before your assessment date. It is important that you take the time to read these thoroughly and understand them, as you will be assessed against them at every stage.

Resilience
Shows resilience, even in difficult circumstances. Prepared to make difficult decisions and has the confidence to see them through. Shows confidence to perform own role without unnecessary support in normal circumstances. Acts in an appropriate way and controls emotions.

As a police community support officer you need to be mentally and physically resilient. Many situations you deal with involve a certain level of stress. You need to be able to cope with it when it happens and to deal with any aftermath.

WHAT IS INVOLVED AT THE SELECTION CENTRE?

At the assessment centre you will be required to undertake two 20-minute written exercises, two interactive/role-play exercises and a competency-based interview, this is the national standard, however some Police services include extra criteria such as Numerical and Verbal reasoning. Always check with the service you are joining for the exact assessment tests you will likely face on the day.

In the written and interactive exercises, you will have to assume a fictitious role and deal with two scenarios. During the interview you will be asked questions about how you have dealt with situations in your past. I have provided you with in-depth information to help you pass this stage in the Interview section of this guide. Before you attend the centre you will be given an information pack and you must read and familiarise yourself with all of its content. Now that you have a brief understanding of the assessable core competencies, let's take a look at the written tests and how you can prepare for them.

CHAPTER 6

ASSESSMENT CENTRE – THE WRITTEN EXERCISES

During the assessment centre you will be asked to undertake 2 written exercises. The written exercise may be in the form of a report, letter, memo or proposal. When you create a written report, the assessor is looking for a well-structured piece of writing that is logical and relevant. You should demonstrate a good use and understanding of English grammar and not make too many spelling mistakes (a maximum of 10), but your aim should be to make none.

The written report is an area of the assessment process that many people do not think they need to practise. They use their preparation time before their assessment date predominantly looking at the Role-Plays and the Interview. Don't make the same mistake. Spend sufficient time working on your handwriting skills and your ability to construct concise and accurate reports.

On the assessment day you will be allowed 20 minutes to read all of the information provided and create your report. This is not a lot of time, especially if you are not prepared. Therefore it is important that you work fast and accurately. In this section we will show you how to manage this time, so you can gather all the relevant information and put it together in a well-structured and logical report.

During the written assessment you may have to assume the role of a Customer Services Officer of a fictitious retail centre. The report you are asked to create will be for the Centre Manager, or someone similar, based around a specific theme. When you are sent the details of your assessment date, you will also be sent two information packs – Information to Candidates and the Centre Welcome Pack (this is the fictitious centre in where you are a customer service officer).

There now follows an example of the type of exercise you could be given.

WRITTEN REPORT SAMPLE EXERCISE 1

You are the Customer Services Officer for a fictitious retail centre. Your manager has asked you to compile a report based on a new pub that is being opened in the centre. Your manager is meeting with the pub owners in a few days time to discuss a few issues and he wants you to write a report based on the information provided.

The pub owners have requested that the pub is open to serve alcohol beverages in the centre from 11am until 11pm.

At the bottom of this page there is a survey sheet, which tells you that, on the whole, the general public and staff are not happy with the idea of a pub being opened in the shopping centre because of perceived antisocial behavioural problems, littering and rowdiness.

It is your job to create a report stating what the main issues are and what your recommendations would be.

SURVEY SHEET FOR SAMPLE EXERCISE 1

The following information has been taken from a survey, which was conducted amongst 100 members of public who regularly shop at the Centre and 30 employees who work at the Centre.

• 60% of the general public and 80% of employees felt that the opening of a pub in the centre would increase littering.

• 80% of the general public and 60% of employees thought that rowdiness in the Centre would increase as a result of the pub opening.

• 10% of the general public and 10% of employees thought that the opening of the pub would be a good idea.

On the following page there is an example of how the report could be written. There are many different recommendations that could have been made.

You should consider the information you have gathered and make the recommendation(s) you consider to be the best for those circumstances.

Remember: recommendations are suggestions for actions or changes.

They should be specific rather than general. It is important that you answer the question and state what your main findings and recommendations are.

SAMPLE RESPONSE TO WRITTEN REPORT EXERCISE 1

From: The Customer Services Officer
To: The Centre Manager
Subject: New pub

Sir,

Please find detailed my findings and recommendations in relation to the new pub as requested. The survey conducted took into consideration the views and opinions of 100 members of the public and 30 members of staff who work at the Centre.

Whilst a small proportion of staff and public (10%) felt that the opening of the pub would be a good idea, the majority of people surveyed felt that there would be problems with antisocial behaviour, littering and rowdiness. Having taken into consideration all of the information provided, I wish to make the following recommendations:

The level of customer service that the centre currently provides is high and it is important that this is maintained. It is important to take into consideration the views and opinions of our customers and staff and to see things from their point of view. I believe that there would be a high risk involved if we were to allow the pub to serve alcoholic beverages from 11am until 11pm and problems with antisocial behaviour could develop. We have a responsibility to protect the public and to ensure that they are safe whilst in the centre.

Whilst it is important to initially obtain the views of the pub owners, I recommend that the pub is only permitted to serve alcoholic beverages from 11am until 1pm and from 5pm until 7pm so as to reduce the risk of the above problems developing.

I have recommended this course of action, as I believe it is in the best interests of the centre, its staff and more importantly our valued customers. This alternative course of action would be for a trial period only and providing there were no problems with antisocial behaviour, littering or rowdiness, we could look to review the opening hours with a view to extending them. I am prepared to take full responsibility for monitoring the situation once the pub has been opened.

The Customer Services Officer

Now that you have read the sample response, take a look at the following information, which will provide you with tips and advice on how to structure and create a response to the written report.

HOW TO CONSTRUCT A RESPONSE – STEP 1

Step one is to read all of the information and documentation quickly and accurately, and then identify what information provided is of importance.

So, what is the important information for this particular exercise? We have highlighted it in bold text for you. Some you will find obvious, some may not be so easy.

SAMPLE EXERCISE 1 – Important Information

You are the Customer Services Officer for a fictitious retail centre. Your manager has asked you to compile a report based on a **new pub** that is being opened in the centre.

Your manager is meeting with the pub owners in a few days time to discuss a few issues and he wants you to write a report based on the information provided. The pub owners have requested that the pub is open to **serve alcohol beverages in the centre from 11am until 11pm.**

On the following page a survey sheet is provided, which tells you that, on the whole, the general public and staff are not happy with the idea of a pub being opened in the shopping centre because of **perceived antisocial behavioural problems, littering and rowdiness.**

It is your job to create a report stating what the main issues are and what your recommendations would be.

Survey Sheet

The following information has been taken from a survey, which was conducted amongst **100 members of the public** who regularly shop at the Centre and **30 employees** who work at the Centre.

- **60% of the general public** and 80% of employees felt that the opening of a pub in the centre would increase littering.

- **80% of the general public** and 60% of employees thought that rowdiness in the Centre would increase as a result of the pub opening.

- **10% of the general public** and 10% of employees thought that the opening of the pub would be a good idea.

Why are these details important?

- Your manager is going to discuss the matter with the pub owners.

- The opening hours may be important, as the centre closes at a specific time (as detailed in the centre welcome pack).

- The plan is to sell alcoholic beverages for a 12-hour period whilst the shopping centre is open.

- The details of the perceived problems are important, as this is what people are worried may occur.

- The number of people surveyed is important to support the percentages used in the statistics.

- The 80% of the general public etc., is the most important figure because customers' views are the most important in this case, as they shop in the centre. Customer focus is very important.

- The 10% of the general public etc., is useful to show that only a small percentage support the idea.

HOW TO CONSTRUCT A RESPONSE – STEP 2

Step two is to plan the structure of your report so it has a beginning, middle and an end. This shows you how the sample report breaks down into these three sections.

From: The Customer Services Officer
To: The Centre Manager
Subject: New pub

Sir,
Please find detailed my findings and recommendations in relation to the new pub as requested. The survey conducted took into consideration the views and opinions of 100 members of the public and 30 members of staff who work at the Centre.

Whilst a small proportion of staff and public (10%) felt that the opening of the pub would be a good idea, the majority of people surveyed felt that there would be problems with antisocial behaviour, littering and rowdiness.

Having taken into consideration all of the information provided, I wish to make the following recommendations:

The level of customer service that the centre currently provides is high and it is important that this is maintained. It is important to take into consideration the views and opinions of our customers and staff and to see things from their point of view. I believe that there would be a high risk involved if we were to allow the pub to serve alcoholic beverages from 11am until 11pm and problems with antisocial behaviour could develop. We have a responsibility to protect the public and to ensure that they are safe whilst in the centre.

Whilst it is important to initially obtain the views of the pub owners, I recommend that the pub is only permitted to serve alcoholic beverages from 11am until 1pm and from 5pm until 7pm so as to reduce the risk of the above problems developing.

I have recommended this course of action, as I believe it is in the best interests of the centre, its staff and more import-antly our valued customers. This alternative course of action would be for a trial period only and providing there were no problems with antisocial behaviour, littering or rowdiness, we could look to review the opening hours with a view to extending them. I am prepared to take full responsibility for monitoring the situation once the pub has been opened.

The Customer Services Officer

Here is a brief description of what should be in each section.

Beginning
Give a brief introduction, saying what the report is about. Explain what has been done and give a short, logical explanation of your findings.

Middle
Here you will write your main findings and recommendations. Remember to include keywords and phrases that you have learnt from the core competencies.

End
This is the summary and conclusion. Say why you have recommended this course of action. Are there any further recommendations? If you are expecting there to be feedback, explain how you propose to deal with this.

IMPORTANT TIPS TO HELP YOU STRUCTURE A GOOD REPORT

• Make the report concise, relevant and easy to read.

• Be sure that your report answers the question that is being asked.

• Limit the number of spelling and grammar errors.

• Create your report using a beginning, middle and an end.

• Use keywords and phrases from the core competencies. This is how the police will assess you.

• Do not spend too much time reading the information and documentation provided. Spend five minutes maximum reading and digesting the documentation, and then spend at least 15 minutes writing your report.

Now that you know how to create a written report, try the sample exercises on the following pages. We have provided you with a template following each exercise for you to create your report. Don't forget to have a copy of the core competencies next to you when writing your practice reports.

WRITTEN REPORT SAMPLE EXERCISE 2

You are the Customer Services Officer for a fictitious retail centre. Your manager has asked you to compile a report regarding one of the shop owners bringing their dog into the centre on a daily basis.

A number of shop owners have reported this matter to the centre manager, as they are not happy about it.

From information gathered, this has been going on for about 6 weeks. There is CCTV footage showing the dog arriving on a number of occasions.

One shop owner reported the dog coming into his shop and fouling. There have also been a further four reports of the dog causing a nuisance and fouling in the centre.

Your job is to review all of the information available and create a report to the centre manager stating what the main issues are and what your recommendations would be to resolve this matter.

Use the template on the following page to create your response.

WRITTEN REPORT SAMPLE EXERCISE 2 TEMPLATE

From:

To:

Title:

WRITTEN REPORT SAMPLE EXERCISE 3

You are the Customer Services Officer for a fictitious retail centre. Your manager has asked you to compile a report regarding the Police Community Action Team patrolling the centre for a period of 5 days, in an attempt to apprehend a team of shoplifters.

The police officers will be in plain clothes. They will be working in partnership with the store detectives that work in the centre. There will be 4 police officers and 5 store detectives. All officers and store detectives will be in radio contact.

The shop owners have been complaining about the steep increase in stock losses over the past 3 months.

Your manager is keen to support this initiative and would like to recommend ways the centre could assist. You are to create a report detailing the main issues and make any recommendations of how you could utilise any of your technology or staff, in order to assist with this initiative.

Use the template on the following page to create your response.

WRITTEN REPORT SAMPLE EXERCISE 3 TEMPLATE

From:

To:

Title:

WRITTEN REPORT SAMPLE EXERCISE 4

You are the Customer Services Officer for a fictitious retail centre. Your manager Mike Meehan has asked you to compile a report regarding an animal rights organisation collecting for their charity in the centre.

The charity would like to collect over a 7-day period, and have a stand on each floor, highlighting the suffering of animals during drug trials. They also want to collect signatures for a petition to ban animal testing.

Your manager is meeting with the charity trustees next week to discuss this matter and he wants you to compile a report based on the information provided.

Statistics obtained from reputable websites show:

- 1 in 3 people support the ban of animal testing.

- 1 in 5 people think animal testing is important.

The charity raises £1.2 million a year through fundraising and has some high profile celebrity supporters.

35 shops in the Centre sell medical and other goods that have been tested on animals. It is your job to create a report stating what the main issues are and what your recommendations would be.

Use the template on the following page to create your response.

WRITTEN REPORT SAMPLE EXERCISE 4 TEMPLATE

From:
To:
Title:

WRITTEN REPORT SAMPLE EXERCISE 5

You are the Customer Services Officer for a fictitious retail centre. Your manager has asked you to compile a report regarding the shopkeepers organising a 'fun day' on the centre grounds for the children from the local special school.

Your manager is in favour of the event, but is worried about safety and security matters. He is meeting with the group of shopkeepers who are coordinating the event next week and would like some further information.

The event is planned to take place in the centre car park. It is anticipated 50 children from the local special school will be attending, together with 10 teachers/staff. Two of the children are in wheelchairs. The local police are keen to support the event, but can only provide one police officer. The local newspaper would also like to cover the 'fun day' taking lots of photographs.

The school is the designated charity of the shopkeepers and if this day is successful they would like to make it an annual event.

You are to create a report stating what the main issues are and what your recommendations would be.

Use the template on the following page to create your response.

WRITTEN REPORT SAMPLE EXERCISE 5 TEMPLATE

From:

To:

Title:

WRITTEN REPORT SAMPLE EXERCISE 6

You are the Customer Services Officer for a fictitious retail centre. Your manager has asked you to review the information he has gathered regarding an accident that occurred in the centre yesterday, when evidence of drug use was found in the gents toilets on the first floor.

A member of the maintenance team found two pieces of foil that were burnt on one side, a used syringe and a tourniquet. A group of youths were reported to be hanging around the toilet area during the afternoon by the neighbouring shops. Other youths were seen to stop and speak to one particular member from the group and it appeared an exchange might have taken place. The eyewitness could not confirm what items were involved in the exchange.

The CCTV from the cameras covering this area has been collected, together with all reports submitted by the security staff, covering the whole day.

Two of the reports state a male youth was seen in the vicinity of the toilets acting in a suspicious manner. They describe him as wearing: a red hooded top (not up), a black bomber-style jacket, very loose black jeans and red trainers. He was the only one of the group wearing red.

The local police have been notified of the drugs paraphernalia and will be attending the centre later today to discuss the incident with the Centre Manager.

You are required to compile a report outlining the main issues and any recommendation you consider appropriate to assist in identifying the youth(s) in an effort to eradicate this activity from the centre.

Use the template on the following page to create your response.

WRITTEN REPORT SAMPLE EXERCISE 6 TEMPLATE

From:

To:

Title:

WRITTEN REPORT SAMPLE EXERCISE 7

You are the customer services officer for a fictitious retail centre. Your manager has asked you to compile a report regarding a number of complaints he has received from shop owners who state that rowdy youths are intimidating shop owners at the centre, which is having a detrimental effect on their business generally and more importantly their takings. Visitor numbers at the centre are down 25% over the last 3 months.

CCTV reports suggest that a gang of 8 youths have been circling the centre during daylight shopping hours, often approaching customers and harassing them for spare change.

The local newspaper have become aware of these incidents and they are sending a reporter along to interview your manager to see what the main problems are and what the centre intends to do about them.

Your report should detail your main findings and also your recommendations as to how the situation can be resolved.

Use the template on the following page to create your response.

WRITTEN REPORT SAMPLE EXERCISE 7 TEMPLATE

From:
To:
Title:

HOW TO CONSTRUCT A LETTER

Now that you have had the opportunity to try out a number of written reports, we will now take a look at how to create a letter or memo.

During the written exercise, you may be required to create a letter or memo that is in response to a complaint or other event whilst assuming the role of a customer services manager. Writing a letter, especially if it is in response to a complaint, can be quite a difficult task. However, with a little bit of preparation and practice you can improve your communication skills greatly.

Try to imagine that you are the manager of a leisure centre or other similar complex. You receive a letter of complaint from a disgruntled member of the public. How do you respond? Obviously you need to be professional and impartial in your response, taking into account the customer's needs following their bad experience. Why do you need to do this? The answer is simple – you are providing a service to that particular customer and they feel you have let them down. Remember how important the core competencies are and what each one stands for!

Of course, it is important to investigate the complaint to ensure its validity but in relation to dealing with complaints you must try to resolve the issue carefully and effectively.

Take a look at the letter of complaint on the following page.

SAMPLE LETTER OF COMPLAINT

Mrs A. Nonymous,
18, Harbour Street,
Newtown, NewPlace.
NW18 YHT

Dear Sir/Madam,

I wish to make a complaint in relation to the service I received at your leisure complex last week. I telephoned your reception to book tickets for a forthcoming concert you are holding at the complex.

My English is not very good and I explained this to the receptionist, as she appeared to be getting impatient with me when I was trying to explain what tickets I wanted. She began to raise her voice quite loud when I asked her to repeat what she had said. In the end she hung up on me due to her impatience. Naturally I feel extremely let down by the service I received that day and won't be using your leisure facilities anymore.

I believe that the receptionist should be told off for her poor handling of the situation and want to know what you are going to do about the matter.

I look forward to hearing from you very soon!

Yours faithfully,

Mrs A. Nonymous.

PREPARING A WRITTEN RESPONSE TO A LETTER

After speaking to the receptionist she admits to becoming impatient with the lady because her English was very poor and it was a very busy day with lots of customers to serve. She says that the telephones kept ringing too and she'd not had a break for over three hours. So you've gathered your information and confirmed that the complaint is a genuine one. How do you deal with it?

You have a number of choices when compiling your response. Do you think it is wise to explain it was a busy period for the receptionist at that time and she had not had a break for a while? The answer should be no.

The problems at the leisure centre in relation to the complaint are purely down to a management issue. There should be enough staff on the reception to deal with the majority of eventualities, including telephone calls, bookings and taking payments, so it is not wise to make any excuses in your letter to the complainant.

When compiling your response you need to think of the core competencies and compose your letter in relation to them. In respect of this particular scenario there is no excuse for the receptionist's behaviour and obviously there is a training issue that needs to be resolved. Your letter, therefore, should reflect the fact that you accept responsibility for the poor customer service the complainant has experienced. On the following page we have compiled a sample response.

SAMPLE RESPONSE TO LETTER OF COMPLAINT

Mr M Rogers,
Leisure Complex Manager,
AAA Leisure Complex,
Swim Street, Gym Town.

Dear Mrs Nonymous,

I am writing in response to your letter of complaint following the service you received at this leisure complex on the 5th November 2009. Following an investigation into the complaint, which I personally conducted, I wish to apologise unreservedly for the poor level of customer service you received on that particular morning. The receptionist failed to provide you with the respect you deserved when dealing with your request to purchase tickets for our forthcoming concert. I fully appreciate how frustrating this must have been for you.

For your information I have formulated a plan to resolve this issue, including retraining to prevent the same happening again to any more of our valued customers. With that in mind I want to thank you for bringing this problem to our attention as without this kind of information we are unable to change or improve the service that we offer.

Once the problem has been resolved I will write to you again to inform you that the issue has been fully rectified. In the meantime I have included 2 complimentary tickets for the forthcoming concert, which I hope you will accept as an offer of apology.

Please contact me on the above telephone number if you have more comments, suggestions or questions.

Yours sincerely,

Mr M Rogers
Leisure Complex Manager

PREPARING A WRITTEN RESPONSE TO A LETTER

After reading the sample response letter do you think it is an appropriate response? The way to ascertain if your responses are correct is to match them against the core competencies relevant to that of a Police Officer.

Whatever letter or response you have to compile during the assessment centre you should always try to match the core competencies, which ultimately means you will have to spend time learning them prior to your assessment centre day.

Everybody has different ways of learning but some of the most effective ways may include:

- Writing the core competencies down every day for 3 weeks prior to your assessment day.

- Reading them at least once every day 3 weeks prior to your assessment day.

- Carrying a small card around with you that has all of the core competencies written out on them. Whenever you have a few minutes spare get the card out and read them.

- Get someone to test you twice a week on the core competencies.

Now try the sample exercise on the following page.

SAMPLE EXERCISE – LETTER WRITING

You are the Customer Services Officer for a fictitious retail centre. Your manager, Mike Meehan, has asked you to compile a report regarding a letter of complaint he has received from a customer, Mr Page.

Mr Page states he was shopping in the centre when a group of youths came past him on skateboards. He says they were smoking and swearing, which he found intimidating. He says the youths are in the centre every afternoon.

This is a copy of Mr Page's letter to Mr Meehan.

Mr J. Page
15 Swale Park Road
Tindale
Shropshire

Dear Mr Meehan,

I am writing to you totally dismayed by the lack of control you have in your centre regarding the rowdy and intimidating youths. I was shopping in the centre on Monday when a group went past me on skateboards, nearly knocking me to the ground. I am 83 years of age and find this behaviour quite intimidating.

If this wasn't bad enough, the youths were smoking and swearing, both of which I understand you say you will not tolerate, but you do not appear to be doing anything to stop it. There was a security guard close by when this occurred, but he did not do anything.

I have even tried to vary my routine in order to avoid these youths, as they appear to be there every afternoon.

Please resolve this matter, or I will have no alternative but to start shopping elsewhere, for my own safety. I would appreciate a response by return.

Yours sincerely

Mr J. Page

Using the templates on the following pages you are required to:

1. Create a report recommending how this matter could be dealt with, addressed to your manager.

2. Write a letter to Mr J. Page responding to his complaint.

WRITTEN REPORT TEMPLATE

From:

To:

Title:

LETTER WRITING TEMPLATE

Mr/Mrs/Ms XXX
Customer Services Officer
AAA Leisure Complex
Swim Street
Gym Town

FINAL TIPS FOR PASSING THE WRITTEN EXERCISES

- In the build up to your assessment practise plenty of report writing.

- Improve your spelling, grammar and punctuation.

- Do not use words that you find hard to spell.

- Make sure your handwriting is neat, tidy and legible.

- Use keywords and phrases from the core competencies.

- Construct your report in a concise manner using a beginning, middle and an end.

- Do not spend too long reading the documentation and paperwork that you are provided with. You need to allocate sufficient time to write your report or letter.

- Before you attend the assessment centre make sure you are fully familiar with the role of the customer services manager and all other associated documentation. There is no excuse for not learning it prior to the day.

CHAPTER 7

ASSESSMENT CENTRE - Numerical & Verbal Reasoning Test

SAMPLE VERBAL AND NUMERICAL REASONING TESTS

As previously mentioned the national standard for PCSO assessment test criteria consists of two 20-minute written exercises, two interactive/role-play exercises and a competency-based interview. However some Police services add extra criteria, to assess a candidates suitability for the role, these can include Numerical and Verbal Reasoning tests. For clarification please check with the service you are applying to join for the exact assessment tests you will face.

To assist you in preparation of these tests, please see sample tests below.

Verbal Reasoning Question number 1

A fire has occurred in a nightclub belonging to Harry James. One person died in the fire, which occurred at 11pm on Saturday night. The club was insured for less than its value.

QUESTIONS – TRUE, FALSE OR IMPOSSIBLE TO SAY?

1. The fire occurred at 1100 hours.

2. A relative of Harry James was killed in the fire.

3. If the insurance company decide to pay out for the fire, Harry James stands to make a profit.

4. The fire was caused by arson.

5. The club was not insured at the time of the fire.

Verbal Reasoning Question number 2

An accident occurred on the M6 motorway between junctions 8 and 9 southbound at 3pm. The driver of a Ford Fiesta was seen to pull into the middle lane without indicating, forcing another car to veer into the central reservation. One person suffered a broken arm and was taken to hospital before the police arrived.

QUESTIONS – TRUE, FALSE OR IMPOSSIBLE TO SAY?

1. The accident was on the M6 motorway on the carriageway that leads to Scotland.

2. The driver of the Ford Fiesta was injured in the crash.

3. The central reservation was responsible for the accident.

4. The police did not give first aid at the scene.

5. The accident happened at 1500 hours.

Verbal Reasoning Question number 3

A man of between 30 and 35 years of age was seen stealing a car from outside Mrs Brown's house yesterday. He was seen breaking the nearside rear window with a hammer before driving off at 40 miles per hour. He narrowly missed a young mother who was pushing a pram.

QUESTIONS – TRUE, FALSE OR IMPOSSIBLE TO SAY?

1. The man who stole the car was 34 years old.

2. He stole Mrs Brown's car.

3. The young mother who was pushing a pram was injured.

4. He used a hammer to smash the windscreen.

5. When he drove off he was breaking the speed limit.

Verbal Reasoning Question number 4

A shopkeeper called Mr Smith was seen serving alcohol to a girl aged 16.

The girl had shown him fake ID, which was a driving licence belonging to her sister. The incident occurred at around 11.30pm on a Wednesday evening during December.

QUESTIONS – TRUE, FALSE OR IMPOSSIBLE TO SAY?

1. The girl is old enough to purchase alcohol from Mr Smith.

2. The girl purchased the alcohol for her sister.

3. The girl's sister had given the driving licence to her.

4. Mr Smith will receive a custodial sentence for his actions.

Verbal Reasoning Question number 5

Following a bank robbery in a town centre, 6 masked gunmen were seen speeding away from the scene in a black van. The incident, which happened in broad daylight in front of hundreds of shoppers, was picked up by CCTV footage. Police are appealing for witnesses. The local newspaper has offered a £5,000 reward for any information leading to the conviction of all the people involved.

QUESTIONS – TRUE, FALSE OR IMPOSSIBLE TO SAY?

1. The car in which the gunmen drove off was a black van.

2. Someone must have seen something.

3. The incident was picked up by CCTV cameras.

4. The newspaper will pay £5,000 for information leading to the arrest of all of the men involved.

5. Police are not appealing to members of the public for help.

Verbal Reasoning Question number 6

A factory fire at 'Stevenage Supplies' was arson, the police have confirmed. A man was seen running away from the scene shortly before the fire started. Earlier that day a man was sacked from the company for allegedly stealing money from the safe. The incident is the second one to occur at the factory in as many months.

QUESTIONS – TRUE, FALSE OR IMPOSSIBLE TO SAY?

1. Police have confirmed that the fire at the factory was arson.

2. The man who was seen running away from the fire was the man who started it.

3. One previous 'fire-related' incident has already occurred at the factory.

4. The man who was sacked from the factory may have started the fire.

Verbal Reasoning Question number 7

At 1800 hours today police issued a statement in relation to the crime scene in Armstrong Road. Police have been examining the scene all day and reports suggest that it may be murder. Forensic officers have been visiting the incident and inform us that the whole street has been cordoned off and nobody will be allowed through. Police say that the street involved will be closed for another 18 hours and no access will be available to anyone during this time.

QUESTIONS – TRUE, FALSE OR IMPOSSIBLE TO SAY?

1. Police have confirmed the incident is murder.

2. Forensic officers have now left the scene.

3. The road will be open at 12 noon the following day.

4. Although the street has been cordoned off, taxis and buses will be given access.

5. Forensic officers will be at the scene all night.

Verbal Reasoning Question number 8

Mrs Rogers telephoned the police at 8pm to report a burglary at her house in Gamble Crescent. She reports that she came home from work and her front bedroom window was open but she doesn't remember leaving it open. She informs the police that her jewellery box is missing and also £40 cash, which was left on the kitchen table. She came home from work at 5pm and left again at 7am in the morning. No other signs of forced entry were visible.

QUESTIONS – TRUE, FALSE OR IMPOSSIBLE TO SAY?

1. The burglar made his/her way in through the bedroom window.

2. The burglar took the jewellery and £40 cash before leaving.

3. Mrs Rogers was away from the house for 10 hours in total.

4. Mrs Rogers may have left the window open herself before leaving for work.

5. There were other visible signs of forced entry.

Verbal Reasoning Question number 9

The local bank was held up at gunpoint on Monday the 18th of September at approximately 4pm. The thieves used a black motorcycle to make their getaway. The following facts are also known about the incident:

- Two shots were fired.

- There were 12 staff members on duty at the time of the raid.

- The alarm was raised by the manager and the police were called.

- The cashier was ordered to hand over a bag of money containing £7,000.

- The thieves have not yet been caught.

- Police are appealing for witnesses.

QUESTIONS – TRUE, FALSE OR IMPOSSIBLE TO SAY?

1. The thieves have been caught.

2. The cashier raised the alarm.

3. The cashier was shot.

4. Two people were injured.

5. The bank was open for business at the time of the

Verbal Reasoning Question number 10

A father and son were found dead in their two-bedroom flat in Sparsbrook on Sunday evening. They had both been suffocated. The following facts are also known:

- The victims were identified by the police as Mark Webster, 16 years old, and his father, Thomas Webster, 39 years old.

- Thomas was in debt to the sum of £37,000.

- Two men were seen leaving the house at 4pm on Sunday afternoon.

- Two men were seen acting suspiciously in the area on Saturday evening before driving off in a Brown Ford Escort car.

- Thomas had previously contacted the police to express his concerns about his safety following threats from his creditors.

- The house had not been broken into.

QUESTIONS – TRUE, FALSE OR IMPOSSIBLE TO SAY?

1. The people Thomas owed money to could have been responsible for the deaths.

2. The two men seen leaving the house were not responsible for the deaths of Mark Webster and Thomas Webster.

3. The house had been broken into.

4. Neighbours reported two men acting suspiciously in the area on Saturday evening.

5. The people responsible for the deaths drove off in a brown Ford Escort car.

ANSWERS TO VERBAL REASONING QUESTIONS

Question 1

1. False

2. Impossible to say

3. False

4. Impossible to say

5. False

Question 2

1. False

2. Impossible to say

3. False

4. True

5. True

Question 3

1. Impossible to say

2. Impossible to say

3. False

4. False

5. Impossible to say

Question 4

1. False

2. Impossible to say

3. Impossible to say

4. Impossible to say

Question 5

1. True

2. Impossible to say

3. True

4. False

5. False

Question 6

1. True

2. Impossible to say

3. True

4. True

Question 7

1. False

2. Impossible to say

3. True

4. False

5. Impossible to say

Question 8

1. Impossible to say

2. Impossible to say

3. False

4. True

5. False

Question number 9

1. False.

2. False.

3. Impossible to say.

4. Impossible to say.

5. Impossible to say.

Question number 10

1. True.

2. Impossible to say.

3. False.

4. Impossible to say.

5. Impossible to say.

NUMERICAL REASONING TEST:

1. A wallet has been found containing one £20 note, five £5 notes, a fifty pence coin and three 2 pence coins. How much is in the wallet?

Answer

2. Subtract 200 from 500, add 80, subtract 30 and multiply by 2. What number do you have?

Answer

3. A multi-storey car park has 8 floors and can hold 72 cars on each floor. In addition to this there is also allocation for 4 disabled parking spaces per floor. How many spaces are there in the entire car park?

Answer

4. A man saves £12.50 per month. How much would he have saved after 1 year?

Answer

5. If there have been 60 accidents along one stretch of a motorway in the last year, how many on average have occurred each month?

Answer

6. Out of 40,000 applicants only 4,000 are likely to be successful. What percentage will fail?

Answer

7. What percentage of 400 is 100?

Answer

8. Malcolm's shift commences at 0615 hours. If his shift is 10.5 hours long what time will he finish?

Answer

9. If Mary can bake 12 cakes in 2 hours how many will she bake in 10 hours?

Answer

10. If there are 24 hours in the day. How many hours are there in one week?

Answer

11. Susan has 10 coins and gives 5 of them to Steven and the remainder to Alan. Alan gives 3 of his coins to Steven who in turn gives half of his back to Susan. How many is Susan left with?

Answer

12. Add 121 to 54. Now subtract 75 and multiply by 10. What is the result?

Answer

13. Ahmed leaves for work at 8am and arrives at work at 9.17am. He then leaves work at 4.57pm and arrives back at home at 6.03pm. How many minutes has Ahmed spent travelling?

Answer

14. A car travels at 30 km/h for the first hour, 65km/h for the second hour, 44 km/h for the third hour and 50 km/h for the fourth hour. What is the car's average speed over the 4-hour journey?

Answer

15. Your friends tell you their electricity bill has gone up from £40 per month to £47 per month. How much extra are they now paying per year?

A	B	C	D	E
£84	£85	£83	£86	£82

16. A woman earns a salary of £32,000 per year. How much would she earn in 15 years?

A	B	C	D	E
£280,000	£380,000	£480,000	£260,000	460,000

17. If a police officer walks the beat for 6 hours at a pace of 4km/h, how much ground will she have covered after the 6 hours is over?

A	B	C	D	E
20km	21km	22km	23km	24km

18. It takes Malcolm 45 minutes to walk 6 miles to work. At what pace does he walk?

A	B	C	D	E
7 mph	4 mph	6 mph	5 mph	8 mph

19. Ellie spends 3 hours on the phone talking to her friend abroad. If the call costs 12 pence per 5 minutes, how much does the call cost in total?

A	B	C	D	E
£3.30	£4.32	£3.32	£4.44	£3.44

20. A woman spends £27 in a retail store. She has a discount voucher that reduces the total cost to £21.60. How much discount does the voucher give her?

A	B	C	D	E
5%	10%	15%	20%	25%

21. A group of 7 men spend £21.70 on a round of drinks. How much does each of them pay if the bill is split evenly?

A	B	C	D	E
£3.00	£65.10	£3.10	£3.15	£3.20

22. 45,600 people attend a football match to watch Manchester United play Tottenham Hotspur. If there are 32,705 Manchester United supporters at the game, how many Tottenham Hotspur supporters are there?

A	B	C	D	E
12,985	13,985	12, 895	12,895	14, 985

23. The police are called to attend a motorway accident involving a coach full of passengers. A total of 54 people are on board, 17 of whom are injured. How many are not injured?

A	B	C	D	E
40	39	38	37	36

24. A car journey usually takes 6 hrs and 55 minutes, but on one occasion the car stops for a total of 47 minutes. How long does the journey take on this occasion?

A	B	C	D	E
6 hrs 40 mins	5 hrs 45 mins	7 hrs 40 mins	7 hrs 42 mins	6 hrs 42 mins

25. There are 10 people in a team. Five of them weigh 70 kg each and the remaining 5 weigh 75 kg each. What is the average weight of the team?

A	B	C	D	E
72.5 kg	71.5 kg	70.5 kg	72 kg	71 kg

ANSWERS TO NUMERICAL REASONING QUESTIONS

1. £45.56

2. 700

3. 608

4. £150

5. 5

6. 90%

7. 25%

8. 1645 hours or 4.45pm

9. 60 cakes

10. 168

11. 4

12. 1000

13. 143 minutes

14. 47.25 km/h

15. A. £84

16. C. £480,000

17. E. 24km

18. E. 8mph

19. B. £4.32

20. D. 20%

21. C. £3.10

22. D. 12,895

23. D. 37

24. D. 7 hrs 42 minutes

25. A. 72.5 kg

CHAPTER 8

ASSESSMENT CENTRE THE ROLE-PLAY EXERCISES

During the PCSO selection centre you will be required to undertake 2 role-play exercises. Most candidates are very nervous about the role-play exercises but there really is no need to feel like this providing you remember to remain calm and focus on the core competencies.

Prior to the role-play exercises you will be provided with a very thorough brief. This is an ideal time to ask any questions that you may have.

The exercises take the following format:

Preparation phase (5 minutes)
During the preparation phase you are allowed 5 minutes in which to read all of the information provided. During this time you will be required to sit at a desk immediately outside the role-play room.

Here, you will read all of the information provided and you will be permitted to take notes on the subject matter in order to assist you.

During the 5 minutes preparation phase it is important to read all of the facts. What are the main issues surrounding the incident? What are the company policies that relate to the incident? What levels of customer service are expected?

Once the 5 minutes of the preparation phase are over you will then go into the activity phase of the role-play.

You will be permitted to take your notes into the role-play and make reference to them but you will not be able to take any writing implements with you.

Activity phase (5 minutes)
When you walk into the room there will be a role-play actor and also at least one role-play assessor. Do not worry about

the assessors but try to focus on the task in hand. During the role-play activity the assessor will normally be sat down throughout the whole duration of the exercise.

The type of scenario that you may be presented with is as follows:

ACTIVITY PHASE EXAMPLE SCENARIO 1

You are the customer services manager for a fictitious retail centre. A lady has made a complaint about an incident that occurred two weeks ago. Six youths barged into her and her daughter whilst they were leaving a shop, leaving them shocked and shaken. The lady states that the youths were drunk and acting in a yobbish manner.

During the role-play exercise it is important to assume the role of the customer services manager and deal with the situation efficiently and effectively. You will need to establish the facts of the incident and take the necessary course of action as required. For example, the above sample scenario will require you to be sensitive, considerate and understanding whilst providing a solution to the problem. You will need to ask questions about the incident and make suggestions as to how you might resolve the issue for them.

I have now provided you with a number of questions and comments that could be used by a candidate who has to deal with this scenario.

ACTIVITY PHASE EXAMPLE SCENARIO 1 – SAMPLE RESPONSES

'Good afternoon, I am the customer services manager and I am here to help you. Could you please start off by telling me

what the problem is?'

'That must have been very distressing for you?'

'How are you now and is your daughter okay following the shock of the incident?'

'I can assure you that we will do all that we can to resolve the issue and I will take personal responsibility for ensuring this happens.'

'Can you tell me what the youths looked like, where they were and at what time the incident occurred?'

'In order to resolve the issue I will take a look at the centre's CCTV cameras to see if we can spot the youths. In the meantime I will keep you informed as to any progress and can only apologise for the distress that has been caused.'

'I can assure you that the centre will not tolerate such behaviour and the matter has been brought to the attention of the Police.'

'Are you happy with my actions and is there anything else I can do to help?'

You will see from the above responses that the candidate is totally focused on the customer at all times. Let's take a look at how he meets the core competencies:

'Good afternoon, I am the customer services manager and I am here to help you. Could you please start off by telling me what the problem is?'

During this opening statement he introduces himself and reassures the customer that he is here to help her. This demonstrates good customer focus. He then goes on to ask his first question, which is designed to gather information, which in turn will allow him to make good decisions. Whilst the customer responds to the question it is important that he demonstrates effective listening skills by nodding his head and generally looking interested and concerned.

'That must have been very distressing for you?'

Whilst this is only one sentence it is designed to demonstrate that the candidate is totally focused on the customer and is concerned for her welfare.

'How are you now and is your daughter okay following the shock of the incident?'

By making reference to the customer's daughter the candidate is demonstrating a good level of understanding of the incident. Again, this demonstrates good customer focus.

'I can assure you that we will do all that we can to resolve the issue and I will take personal responsibility for ensuring this happens.'

During this statement the candidate demonstrates the core competency of personal responsibility.

'Can you tell me what the youths looked like, where they were and at what time the incident occurred?'

The candidate is now starting to gather evidence so that he can problem solve.

'In order to resolve the issue I will take a look at the centre's CCTV cameras to see if we can spot the youths. In the meantime I will keep you informed as to any progress and can only apologise for the distress that has been caused.'

The candidate is demonstrating effective communication

and is keeping the customer updated on what he intends to do. He apologises for the distress caused, which in turn demonstrates good customer focus.

'I can assure you that the centre will not tolerate such behaviour and the matter has been brought to the attention of the Police.'

During this statement he is demonstrating his awareness of the centre's policy relating to bullying and harassment. Without this knowledge, which has been gained by reading the policy, he would not be able to provide a suitable solution to the problem. He is also demonstrating the core competency of respect for race and diversity.

'Are you happy with my actions and is there anything else I can do to help?'

The candidate now confirms that the customer is satisfied, thus demonstrating once again a good level of customer service.

Now that you are starting to gain an understanding of what is required during the role-play exercises, take a look at the following tips, which will help you to gain higher scores.

TIPS FOR PASSING THE ROLE-PLAY EXERCISES

- Read all of the information thoroughly during the 5 minutes preparation phase. Take notes that are concise and relevant. For example:

  1. What is the centre's policy on drinking alcohol?
  2. What is the centre's policy on customer service?
  3. What is the centre's policy on fairness and equality?

- Once you have read all of the information and compiled your notes, prepare yourself for the activity phase.

- Remember to stay calm, be polite and courteous at all times and do not get defensive or angry.

- Ask probing questions in order to establish the facts.

- Tell the person/people making the complaint what the centre's policy is regarding the issue.

- Reassure them if necessary and tell them what your plan of action is in order to resolve the issue.

- Tell them that you will keep them informed of all progress.

- Use keywords and phrases from the core competencies when communicating with the role-play actor. For example – *'I will take personal responsibility for resolving this issue.'*

- Challenge any behaviour that is either discriminatory or inappropriate, but never lose your temper or become confrontational.

- Ask them if they are satisfied with your actions so far and if there is anything else you can do to help them.

Now take a look at the sample role-play exercises that I have provided on the following pages. How would you deal with them? Following each sample scenario I have provided you with a box to make notes. Use the box provided to make notes on how you would deal with the scenario in line with the core competencies.

ACTIVITY PHASE EXAMPLE SCENARIO 2

You are the customer services manager for a fictitious retail centre.

A special needs carer has made a complaint stating that Mary (the girl he cares for) was recently treated unfairly by a security guard at the centre when she informed him that she had lost her purse.

Allegedly, the security guard refused to search for Mary's purse.

The security guard states in his report that this is the third time Mary has complained about losing her purse when all the time it was in her handbag.

The carer is angry and wants the security guard to be investigated.

Suggestions for dealing with the scenario

- Remember to focus on providing a high level of service at all times.

- Ask the carer if Mary is OK and whether you can do anything to reassure her.

- Apologise for the poor level of customer service.

- Ask plenty of questions in order to establish the facts. Where/when did the incident occur? Is there a description of the security guard? What did he say or do?

- Make use of the facilities at the centre in order to gather more information, e.g. CCTV cameras.

- Inform the carer that any form of bullying, harassment or inappropriate behaviour will not be tolerated at the centre in accordance with the policy.

- Provide a suitable solution to the problem. You may wish to consider re-training for the security guard if it transpires following your investigation that he is guilty of the alleged inappropriate action.

ACTIVITY PHASE EXAMPLE SCENARIO 2 – YOUR NOTES

ACTIVITY PHASE EXAMPLE SCENARIO 3

You are the customer services manager for a fictitious retail centre.

A member of staff would like to speak to you regarding an incident of alleged bullying. He claims that over the last three months another member of staff has been making inappropriate comments relating to his sexual orientation.

He is very upset about the incident and wants you to sort it out.

You are to gather the facts and decide on the most appropriate course of action to take.

Suggestions for dealing with the scenario
- Read the core competency that relates to respect for diversity and integrity.

- Remember that no form of bullying or harassment is tolerated.

- During the preparation phase, read the equality policy. Make sure you make reference to it during the activity phase. For example:

  'I understand that this must be extremely distressing for you. I can assure you that no form of bullying or harassment will be tolerated at this centre. The equality policy states...'

- Demonstrate a level of empathy when dealing with the situation. The core competency of 'customer focus' is still relevant in scenarios where you are dealing with employees of the centre.

- Make sure you ask appropriate questions and gather the facts about the alleged incident. When did this/these incident(s) occur? Who is the alleged guilty person? What exactly was said? Has the person challenged the alleged offender or asked them to stop?

- Follow the steps that are provided in the equality policy when making your decision.

ACTIVITY PHASE EXAMPLE SCENARIO 3 – YOUR NOTES

ACTIVITY PHASE EXAMPLE SCENARIO 4

You are the customer services manager for a fictitious retail centre.

A member of the public wants to see you regarding an issue that occurred at the centre recently. She claims that, despite the centre having 200 parking spaces for disabled badge holders, ordinary members of the public are using the parking spaces without a permit.

Just the other day she had to park in a space 200 yards from the entrance and she is not happy about it.

You are to gather the facts of the alleged incident and deal with it in an appropriate manner.

Suggestions for dealing with the scenario

- Read the welcome pack thoroughly before you attend the assessment centre. This will give you details relating to this type of scenario.

- If the centre is at fault then you must admit it and apologise for the poor level of customer service.

- Show a level of empathy and understanding by saying something like:

  'I understand that this must be very inconvenient for you. I apologise unreservedly for this incident. I can assure you that steps will be taken to improve this situation and I will take personal responsibility for making sure that improvements are made.'

  You will notice in the above example response that I have used the words 'personal responsibility'. This is one of the assessable core competencies.

- Demonstrate a level of empathy when dealing with the

situation. The core competency of 'customer focus' is still relevant in scenarios where you are dealing with employees of the centre.

- Make sure you ask appropriate questions and gather the facts about the alleged incident. When did the incident occur? Has this been a regular thing?

- Remember to make use of the facilities that are available to you at the centre. You may decide to use the CCTV cameras in order to find out who has been using the car parking spaces illegally.

- Your resolution might involve carrying out an internal investigation to assess why this incident has occurred. If you do this, be sure to tell the lady that you will keep her informed of any progress.

- In order to prevent the incident from occurring again, you may decide to ask a security guard to carry out hourly checks in the car park in order to keep the spaces available for disabled users.

ACTIVITY PHASE EXAMPLE SCENARIO 4 – YOUR NOTES

ACTIVITY PHASE EXAMPLE SCENARIO 5

You are the customer services manager for a fictitious retail centre.

A member of the public wants to see you about an incident that has just occurred at the centre. Whilst shopping, his daughter disappeared from his side and he is extremely worried and distressed.

He wants you to find her as soon as possible.

You are to gather the facts of the incident and deal with it in an appropriate manner.

Suggestions for dealing with the scenario

- This type of situation assesses your ability to remain calm, yet act quickly and decisively. As you can imagine, the role actor will be acting in a distressed manner and it will be your job to calm them down so that you can establish the facts and make the correct decision. It is crucial that you provide a very high level of customer service.

- Once you have calmed the customer down you will need to quickly gather the facts. This might include details relating to his daughter's appearance, what she was wearing, where she was last seen, what shops she likes at the centre, where he thinks she may have gone etc.

- Once you have gathered the facts you may decide to:

  Make a tannoy announcement asking the girl to make her way to the nearest customer services desk;

  Inform all members of staff that the girl is missing, provide them with a description and ask them to search for her;

Inform the Police immediately so they can assist in the search;

Post a security guard at each exit to prevent the girl from leaving the centre and wandering off onto the dangerous roads.

- Throughout the activity phase make sure you sympathise with the customer and provide a high level of customer service. For example:

'I understand that this must be very distressing for you sir but I can assure you that we will do everything we can to find her quickly, and return her to you both safe and well.'

ACTIVITY PHASE EXAMPLE SCENARIO 5 – YOUR NOTES

ACTIVITY PHASE EXAMPLE SCENARIO 6

You are the customer services manager for a fictitious retail centre.

One of the centre store managers wants to see you about a gang of youths who are standing outside his shop behaving in an antisocial manner, swearing and obstructing customers from entering his shop.

He is very annoyed at the situation and is losing money because potential customers are not allowed to shop in comfort without feeling threatened.

Suggestions for dealing with the scenario

- To begin with you should study the 'OPERATIONS' information and the 'CODE OF CONDUCT' information in the Welcome Pack. What do they say that possibly relates to the above scenario? Is this kind of behaviour tolerated? Can people who behave in such a manner be escorted from the centre and should the police be involved? Can you involve the security staff or use the CCTV cameras to provide the police with evidence?

- Remember that the manager is annoyed at the situation and therefore you may have to defuse a confrontational situation in the first instance. Remember to be firm but stay calm and never become confrontational yourself.

ACTIVITY PHASE EXAMPLE SCENARIO 6 – YOUR NOTES

ACTIVITY PHASE EXAMPLE SCENARIO 7

You are the customer services manager for a fictitious retail centre.

A customer would like to see you about an issue surrounding a dog that is in the shopping centre. She is very annoyed that a dog has been allowed to enter the shopping centre and wants to know what you are going to do about it.

The dog is an 'assistance dog' for a visually impaired customer.

Suggestions for dealing with the scenario

• To begin with you should study the 'OPERATIONS' information, the 'CODE OF CONDUCT' information and the 'EQUALITY POLICY' statement relating to the centre. What do they say that possibly relates to the above scenario? Are 'assistance dogs' permitted? If the answer is 'yes' then the person may not have any grounds for complaint. However, it is important to listen to the complaint before responding in a calm but firm manner.

• Remember to be confident/resilient in your handling of the situation and refer to the policy of the centre for such issues. Do not get drawn into personal opinions but stick to the code of conduct for the centre and apply it accordingly.

ACTIVITY PHASE EXAMPLE SCENARIO 7 – YOUR NOTES

FINAL TIPS FOR PASSING THE ROLE-PLAY SCENARIOS

- Learn the welcome pack prior to attending the assessment. This will allow you to focus on the scenario and how you intend to deal with it during the preparation phase.

- Always remain calm during every scenario. Never lose your temper or become confrontational. If you do, you will probably fail.

- Try to deal with the role actor in a sensitive and considerate manner.

- It is vital that you challenge any behaviour that is either bullying or inappropriate. Make reference to the equality policy during incidents of this nature.

- Use the information contained within the welcome pack to deal with all situations. There are things there to assist you such as CCTV cameras, a Police station and a tannoy system to name just a few.

- Focus on providing a high level of customer service at all times.

- Use keywords and phrases from the core competencies when dealing with the role actor. Here are just a few examples:

  'I can assure you that I will take personal responsibility for resolving this issue.' PERSONAL RESPONSIBILITY

  'My aim is to sort out this problem as quickly as possible.' COMMUNITY AND CUSTOMER FOCUS

  'I must apologise for the mistakes that we have made.' COMMUNITY AND CUSTOMER FOCUS

'Are you satisfied with the service I have provided?'
COMMUNITY AND CUSTOMER FOCUS

'The centre's policy that relates to this issue is....'
PROBLEM SOLVING

'Before I make a decision I want to consider all of the facts.' RESILIENCE

'I fully understand that you might not be happy with my decision, but that is the stance I am going to take.'
RESILIENCE

'Yes, I can certainly see that from your point of view.'
RESPECT FOR RACE AND DIVERSITY

'I understand that this must be very difficult for you.'
RESPECT FOR RACE AND DIVERSITY

'I can assure you that I will treat this information in confidence as requested.'
RESPECT FOR RACE AND DIVERSITY

'I must ask you to stop using that form of language sir.'
RESPECT FOR RACE AND DIVERSITY

'Is there any way that I can help you?'
TEAM WORKING

After carefully studying the core competencies you may find that there are other phrases and keywords that you can use. This is a great approach to use and you will be able to use many of the phrases during each role-play. The most important factor is to make sure you hit each of the assessable core competencies.

CHAPTER 9

ASSESSMENT CENTRE - THE INTERVIEW

INTRODUCTION

The PCSO interview forms part of the assessment centre. It is different to that of a 'normal' job interview in the fact that it assesses your ability to meet a number of core competencies. The interview panel will normally comprise of one or two people and the interview will consist of four competency-based questions over a maximum twenty-minute period.

The interviewer(s) will be dressed in civilian clothes and will be either serving or retired Police Officers or qualified assessors who are not part of the Police Force. Prior to the interview it is essential that you come up with a number of different scenarios that you have experienced, either at work or in your social/personal life, which are based around the assessable core competencies.

The interview is relatively relaxed and is designed to get the most out of the candidate. The interviewer may ask 'probing' questions that are designed to get the information out of you. For example, you may be asked the following initial question:

'Give a scenario when you have had to be considerate to someone else's feelings.'

Further probing questions to this question might be:

'How did they feel?'

'How did you feel at the time?'

'Why did you take this course of action?'

'What was the outcome?'

Before I provide you with a number of sample interview questions and tips on how to answer them, I think it is important to explain how important interview 'technique' is. The majority of candidates will spend all of their time preparing their responses to the interview questions. As a result they will tend to neglect the important area of technique.

Interview technique is basically how you present yourself at interview. Let's take a look at the difference between a 'good' applicant and a 'poor' applicant.

A Good Applicant

A good applicant is someone who has taken the time to prepare. They have researched both the Police Force they are applying to join and also the role that they are being interviewed for. They may not know every detail about the organisation and the role but it will be clear that they have made an effort to find out important facts and information. They will be well presented at the interview and they will be confident, but not over confident. As soon as they walk into the interview room they will be polite and courteous and they will sit down in the interview chair only when invited to do so. Throughout the interview they will sit upright in the chair and communicate in a positive manner. If they do not know the answer to a question they will say so and they won't try to waffle. At the end of the interview they will ask positive questions about the job or the organisation before shaking hands and leaving.

A Poor Applicant

A poor applicant could be any combination of the following. They will be late for the interview or even forget to turn up at all. They will have made little effort to dress smartly and they will have carried out little or no preparation. When asked questions about role they will have little or no knowledge. Throughout the interview they will appear to be unenthusiastic about the whole process and will look as if they want the interview to be over as soon as possible. Whilst sat in the interview chair they will slouch and fidget. At the end of the interview they will try to ask clever questions that are intended to impress the panel.

Earlier on in the guide I made reference to a 'mock interview'. I strongly advise that you try out a mock interview before the real thing. You'll be amazed at how much your confidence will improve. All you need to do is get a friend or a relative to sit down with you and ask you the interview questions that are contained within this guide. Try to answer them as if you were at the real interview. The more mock interviews you try, the more confident you'll become.

Improving Interview Technique
How you present yourself during the interview is important. Whilst assessing candidates for interviews I will not only assess their responses to the interview questions but I will also pay attention to the way they present themselves. A candidate could give excellent responses to the interview questions but if they present themselves in a negative manner then this can lose them marks.

Take a look at the following diagrams, which indicate both poor technique and good technique.

POOR INTERVIEW TECHNIQUE

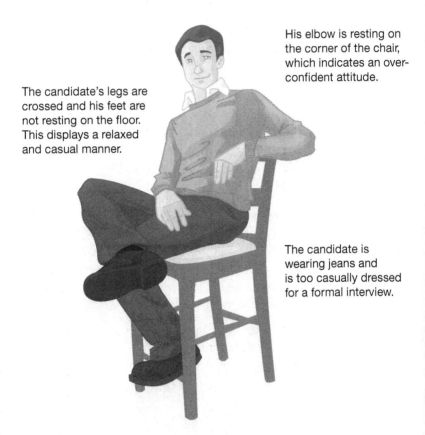

His elbow is resting on the corner of the chair, which indicates an over-confident attitude.

The candidate's legs are crossed and his feet are not resting on the floor. This displays a relaxed and casual manner.

The candidate is wearing jeans and is too casually dressed for a formal interview.

The candidate appears to be too relaxed and casual for an interview.

GOOD INTERVIEW TECHNIQUE

The candidate is smiling
and he portrays a confident,
but not over-confident manner.

The candidate is dressed
wearing a smart suit. It is
clear that he has made an
effort in his presentation.

His hands are in a stable
position, which will prevent
him from fidgeting. He could
also place his hands palms
facing downwards and
resting on his knees.

He is sitting upright
in the interview chair
with his feet resting
on the floor. He is not
slouching and he
portrays himself in a
positive manner.

In the build-up to your interview practise a few mock interviews. Look to improve your interview technique as well as working on your responses to the interview questions.

On the following pages I have provided you with a number of sample questions and also probing questions to assist you during your preparation. You will also note that I have provided a sample response to each question. It is important not to use these responses during your interview, but instead use them as a basis for your own preparation.

Please note that the questions I have provided are not guaranteed to be the ones you will encounter during your interview. The Police Force does change the assessable core competencies from time to time. However, if you follow my advice and create a strong response for every core competency prior to the interview then your chances of success will increase greatly.

SAMPLE QUESTION NUMBER 1
(core competency team working)

Give a scenario where you have had to work as part of a team in order to achieve something.

How to respond to this question
Working as part of a team is very much an integral part of the role of a PCSO. When constructing your response, try to think of a situation where you worked effectively with other people in order to achieve a difficult task. The situation could either be whilst at work, at home or even during a sporting/social event. Have a copy of the core competency next to you and try to use keywords and phrases that match the key positive indicators.

Take a look at the following sample response. I have highlighted the keywords and phrases that I believe match the core competency of team working.

SAMPLE RESPONSE TO QUESTION NUMBER 1
(core competency team working)

'Whilst working in my current role as a sales administrator at a local retail store, we were presented with a difficult task that required a **high standard of team work**. It was only thirty minutes until opening time, when we received a large unexpected stock delivery. We only had thirty minutes to bring the stock into store and check the contents. This kind of task would normally take at least one hour to complete.

I volunteered to work with three other staff members to get the job done before opening time. **We all came together and discussed** quickly how we would approach the team task. It was my job to check the stock as it came in and tick off the check sheet in accordance with company policy.

The other team members had the responsibility of bringing in the stock and storing it in the correct location once I had cleared it.

We all worked collectively as a team and kept in constant communication. *At one point, one of the team members needed a break from lifting,* **so I swapped roles with her so that she could take a break.** *Each team member* **supported** *each other and we kept a constant check on the time.*

The task was completed just in time for store opening. The success of the task was down to the **collective team approach** *and the fact that we* **supported each other** *and kept in constant* **communication.***'*

Whilst preparing the response to the above question it is important that you have a copy of the relevant core competency next to you. You will see that I have used keywords and phrases from the core competency in my response.

Once you have finished your answer to the question, the interviewer may ask you probing questions. Here are a few examples of questions they may ask:

'How did you feel at the time?'
'Did you find it difficult working in the team environment?'
'What did the rest of the team feel about your actions?'
'Why did you take this course of action?'
'What was the end result?'

Now use the template on the following page to create your own response to this question based on your own experiences.

TEMPLATE FOR QUESTION NUMBER 1
(CORE COMPETENCY TEAM WORKING)

Give a scenario where you have had to work as part of a team in order to achieve something.

SAMPLE QUESTION NUMBER 2
(core competency respect for race and diversity)

Give a scenario when you have had to be considerate to someone else's views and/or opinions.

How to respond to this question
It is important to remember that the core competency of respect for race and diversity is assessed heavily during the entire selection process. Therefore, you need to create a response that is targeted at matching the core competency. Society is extremely diverse in nature and you must feel comfortable when working with, and helping, people from different backgrounds and cultures. Of course, it is also vital that you are honest in your response so make sure you choose one that is an accurate reflection of your true feelings.

Take a look at the following sample response. I have highlighted the keywords and phrases that I believe match the core competency of respect for race and diversity.

SAMPLE RESPONSE TO QUESTION NUMBER 2
(core competency respect for race and diversity)

'Whilst working as a sales assistant in my current job, a new member of the team, who was from a different background, started work at the shop.

*Whilst getting to know him, it transpired that he needed to pray at specific times of the day as part of his religious beliefs. The time that he needed to pray coincided with my afternoon break. In order to help him, I volunteered to change my break time so that he could have the time to pray. It was important for me to **see things from his point of view** and to **show understanding** for his situation. This in turn would allow the* *team to work more effectively and it would further strengthen our working relationship.*

I fully understand that **there are a broad range of cultural customs,** *and by offering to help out, I believe that I was* **taking into account his personal needs.'**

Once you have finished your answer to the question, the interviewer may ask you probing questions. Here are a few examples of questions they may ask:

Probing questions:

'Why did you take this course of action?'
'How did you feel at the time?'
'How did they respond to your actions?'

Now use the template on the following page to create your own response to this question based on your own experiences.

TEMPLATE FOR QUESTION NUMBER 2
(RESPECT FOR RACE AND DIVERSITY)

Give a scenario when you have had to be considerate to someone else's views and/or opinions.

SAMPLE QUESTION NUMBER 3
(core competency resilience)

Give a scenario when you have had to show resilience and stick by what you believed.

How to respond to this question
As you can imagine, PCSOs must be confident in a crisis. The members of public whom you are serving will expect you to take control of situations and deal with them in an effective, calm and appropriate manner. This question assesses your ability to do just that.

When responding to the question, try to include keywords such as:

• Confidence

• Calm

• Professional

• Restrained

• Reliable

Now take a look at the following sample response. Once again I have highlighted the keywords and phrases that I believe match the core competency of resilience.

SAMPLE RESPONSE TO QUESTION NUMBER 3
(core competency resilience)

'It was a busy Saturday afternoon and I was working as a temporary manager for a local retail store. All of a sudden the fire alarm began to sound and I immediately implemented the company's policy, which included calling the Fire Service and evacuating the shop. As soon as I started to evacuate

the shop, some members of staff began to question my decision stating that the fire alarm would probably be a false alarm, and there was therefore no need to evacuate.

__I remained calm and in control of the situation__ and instructed them to assist me in evacuating the shop. It was important that I followed company procedures and I also had the safety of my staff and the customers at the forefront of my mind. Even though one or two members of staff continued to question my decision, I __remained professional and restrained__ and insisted that a full evacuation was carried out.

Once the Fire Service arrived they carried out a thorough inspection and found there to be a small fire in one of the storerooms. Once the incident was over, I held a staff meeting and reiterated the importance of following company policies without questioning my decisions or authority. I felt it was important to deal __with the situation in a calm and restrained way.'__

Once you have finished your answer to the question, the interviewer may ask you probing questions. Here are a few examples of questions they may ask:

Probing questions:

'How did it make you feel at the time?'
'Why did you take this course of action?'
'How did the other person(s) respond to your resilience?'
'What was the final outcome?'

Now use the template on the following page to create your own response to this question based on your own experiences.

TEMPLATE FOR QUESTION NUMBER 3 (RESILIENCE)

Give a scenario when you have had to show resilience and stick by what you believed.

SAMPLE QUESTION NUMBER 4
(core competency community and customer focus)

Give a scenario where you have had to deal with a situation where somebody was not happy with a service they had received.

How to respond to this question

This question assesses your ability to provide a high level of customer care. During the role-play scenarios the assessors are looking for you to focus on the customer at all times, and you should adopt the same sort of approach when answering this type of question.

When creating a response to this question, try to include the following areas:

- Focus on the customer at all times

- Find out the facts regarding why the person was not happy

- Apologise for the poor service

- Try to sort out the problem as quickly as possible

- Keep the person updated on progress and any decisions you make

- Check that the person is happy with your resolution

Now take a look at the following sample response. Once again I have highlighted the keywords and phrases that I believe match the core competency of community and customer focus.

SAMPLE RESPONSE TO QUESTION NUMBER 4 (core competency community and customer focus)

'I was working in a shoe shop when an angry customer approached me wishing to make a complaint. I started off by asking him in a polite manner to explain what the problem was. He told me that he had purchased some trainers for his daughter's birthday from the shop a week before. When his daughter opened the box on her birthday, one of the trainers was missing. The shop assistant had forgotten to place one of the trainers in the box at the time of purchase and naturally the customer was very unhappy.

***After I had listened carefully to his complaint I apologised for the poor level of service.** I then set **about rectifying the problem and focused on his needs at all times** during our conservation. I told him that I would refund his payment in full and provide his daughter with a brand new pair of trainers up to the value of £50. **I checked to see that he was satisfied with my offer** and he was. I also informed him that I would be carrying out an investigation to see why this incident occurred with a view to preventing it from happening again in the future. **I told him that I would contact him again to let him know the outcome of my investigation.** He left the shop very happy and thanked me for the high level of service I had provided him with.'*

Once you have finished your answer to the question, the interviewer may ask you probing questions. Here are a few examples of questions they may ask:

Probing questions:

'Why did you take this course of action?'
'How did they respond?'
'What was the final result?'
'How did this make you feel?'

Now use the template on the following page to create your own response to this question based on your own experiences.

TEMPLATE FOR QUESTION NUMBER 4 (COMMUNITY AND CUSTOMER FOCUS)

Give a scenario where you have had to deal with a situation where somebody was not happy with a service they had received.

SAMPLE QUESTION NUMBER 5
(core competency personal responsibility)

Give a scenario where you have taken personal responsibility for making something happen.

How to respond to this question

PCSOs should be good at taking responsibility for making things happen. Whilst they are required to work effectively as part of a team, they are also required to work on their own and are responsible for solving problems and issues. This question will assess your ability to do just that.

When responding to this type of question, try to concentrate on the following areas:

• Taking responsibility for your own actions

• Taking pride in your work

• Displaying initiative

• Following things through to the end

Now take a look at the following sample response. Once again I have highlighted the keywords and phrases that I believe match the core competency of personal responsibility.

SAMPLE RESPONSE TO QUESTION NUMBER 5
(core competency personal responsibility)

'I decided that I wanted to raise money for a local important charity by carrying out a sponsored fitness event. Basically I wanted to raise £10,000 by running a marathon, swimming two miles and then cycling 100 miles, all in one day.

I started off by making a plan of how I was going to get fit for the event and also how I intended raising the money. I set *out an action plan that made sure I trained hard in each of the three areas, and **specifically on improving my weaker areas.** I took **personal responsibility for making sure I met each target area** on a weekly basis, as per my action plan. During the evenings I would go out to local houses in order to raise the sponsors that I needed. I decided to **use my initiative** and I left sponsorship sheets at the checkout tills of my local supermarket. This in itself proved to be a good decision as the majority of sponsorship came from here.*

*After three months of hard preparation and fundraising I managed to complete the fitness event in the set time period and raised just under the target of £10,000. It was important to me that I completed the event as planned, as **I did not want to let the charity down.'***

Once you have finished your answer to the question, the interviewer may ask you probing questions. Here are a few examples of questions they may ask:

Probing questions:

'How did you feel at the time?'
'Did you feel under pressure?'
'What was the end result?'

Now use the template on the following page to create your own response to this question based on your own experiences.

TEMPLATE FOR QUESTION NUMBER 5 (PERSONAL RESPONSIBILITY)

Give a scenario where you have taken personal responsibility for making something happen.

FINAL TIPS FOR PASSING THE PCSO INTERVIEW

- Stronger performing candidates are able to provide specific examples in response to each question.

- Try to think of scenarios, based around the core competencies, that you have encountered in the past, prior to attending the interview.

- When responding to each question, outline your contributions or actions and try to provide evidence of the competency area being assessed.

- Use keywords and phrases from the core competencies when answering the questions. This will allow you to score higher and it will also make the interviewers job easier too!

- Speak clearly, use correct English and structure each response logically.

- Sit up straight in the chair, smile and be polite.

- When responding to the interview questions do not 'generalise' but rather be specific.

CHAPTER 10

ASSESSMENT CENTRE DIARIES

INTRODUCTION

The following information has been supplied by a recent successful PCSO applicant who attended the selection centre.

Arriving at the assessment centre

I was due to start the assessment centre at 1pm so I made sure that I arrived with plenty of time to spare. I parked up in the Police Training Centre car park and sat in the car for 20 minutes reading the PCSO core competencies. This proved to be really effective and it helped me to focus my mind on the requirements of the PCSO role and, more specifically, the areas that I would be assessed against.

At 12.50pm I made my way to the reception area, signed in, and then sat patiently with the other 15 or so candidates who were also there to take the assessments. At 1pm two very polite and helpful ladies entered and introduced themselves as members of the recruitment team. They made us all feel at ease before we made our way to the briefing rooms. At this point we were split into two groups for ease of assessment.

The written assessment

The first test was the written assessment, although this can vary from force to force, so be prepared to take any of the assessments first. We were told that we had 20 minutes to complete the first assessment, which comprised the following:

You are the customer services officer for a fictitious retail centre. Your manager has asked you to compile a report based on a new pub that is being opened in the centre. Your manager is meeting with the pub owners in a few days time to discuss a few issues and he wants you to write a report based on the information provided.

Within the literature you are provided with a survey sheet, which tells you that, on the whole, the general public and staff are not happy with the idea of a pub being opened in the shopping centre because of perceived antisocial behavioural problems, littering and rowdiness. It is your job to create a report stating what the main issues are and what your recommendations would be.

When creating your report, remember the core competencies associated with the PCSO role and structure the report so that you cover the areas required in the question whilst demonstrating the core competencies. State the main issues and then make your recommendations. Once the 20 minutes was up we were told to put down our pens before handing in our responses. Remember to ensure that you have completed the information at the top of each report, including your candidate number and report details.

After a 5-minute break we were straight into the second report. Basically, this was along the same lines as the first report but was based around the different theme of school truancy. Once again you are the customer services officer and your manager has asked you to compile a report. The local School Truancy Enforcement Team would like to spend 5 days in the shopping centre looking for children who are absent from school. They suspect that many of the absent children are spending their time at the shopping centre and they feel that they could reduce truancy levels if they show a presence at the centre.

Within the information provided you will be presented with a report from the School Truancy Enforcement Team, which explains the truancy levels in detail and also the crime/antisocial behavioural problems in the area surrounding the school.

The manager has asked you to create a report based around the following:

- The advantages/disadvantages of the proposal;

- Your recommendations, having taken into consideration all of the facts provided.

When compiling your report, once again remember to keep it relevant to the question. State the advantages/disadvantages and then make your recommendations. Once the 20-minute time period was up we were told to put down our pens before handing in our reports.

TOP TIPS FOR COMPLETING THE WRITTEN REPORTS

- The report could be based around any topic so do not assume that the above two questions are the ones that you will be asked.

- Keep your report concise and relevant, and remember to answer the question.

- Avoid spelling mistakes, as you will lose marks. If you do not want a word or sentence to be assessed then draw a neat line through it.

- Spend a maximum of 5 minutes reading the information provided. Anything over this will leave you little time to complete your report.

THE ROLE-PLAY SCENARIOS

Following the completion of the written assessment, we then had 15 minutes to prepare for the 2 role-play exercises. Most of the candidates were very nervous about the role-play but there really is no need to feel like this providing you remember to remain calm and focus on the core competencies.

Prior to the role-play exercises we were provided with a very thorough brief. This is an ideal time to ask any questions that you may have. Once the brief was complete we were then taken to a waiting room before commencing the role-play exercises. The exercises take the following format:

Preparation Phase
During the preparation phase you are allowed 5 minutes in which to read all of the information provided. During this time I was required to sit at a desk immediately outside the role-play room. Here, I read all of the information provided and took notes on the subject matter to assist me.

The two scenarios that I was presented with are as follows:

Scenario 1
You are the customer services manager for a fictitious retail centre. A lady has made a complaint about an incident that occurred two weeks ago. Six youths barged into her and her daughter whilst they were leaving a shop, leaving them shocked and shaken. The lady states that the youths were drunk and acting in a yobbish manner.

Scenario 2
You are the customer services manager for a fictitious retail centre. A special needs carer has made a complaint stating that Mary (the girl he cares for) was recently treated unfairly by a security guard at the centre when she informed him that she had lost her purse. Allegedly, the security guard refused to search for Mary's purse. The security guard states in his report that this is the third time Mary has complained about losing her purse when all the time it was in her handbag. The carer is angry and wants the security guard to be investigated.

During the 5 minutes preparation phase it is important to read the facts. What are the main issues surrounding the incident? What are the company policies that relate to the incident? What levels of customer service are expected?

Once the 5 minutes of the preparation phase are over you will then go into the activity phase of the role-play. You will be permitted to take your notes into the role-play and make reference to them but you will not be able to take any writing implements with you.

Activity phase

When you walk into the room there will be a role-play actor and also at least one role-play assessor. Do not worry about the assessors but try to focus on the task in hand. During the role-play activity (scenario 1) indicated above, the lady actor was sat down throughout the whole duration of the exercise.

As soon as I walked through the door I introduced myself as the customer services officer and I asked her how I could help. She was very upset that the youths had barged into her and her daughter and she wanted something done about it. She was also angry that the centre had allowed them to drink alcohol on the premises. I started off by asking her if she and her daughter were okay and reassured her that I would deal with the situation as professionally and quickly as possible. I then began to establish the facts by asking the following questions:

- Where and at what time did the incident occur?

- What did the youths look like and what were they wearing?

- How old were they?

Once I established the facts of the incident I explained to her what I was going to do about the issue. I also explained to her the company's policy regarding alcohol consumption on the premises and that this sort of behaviour would not be tolerated. I then informed her that I would contact the local Police to obtain their assistance in resolving the issue. We would check the centre CCTV cameras to see if they picked up the incident and to see if any of the youths were recognisable to the Police. I reassured her that everything would be done to try to resolve the issue and that I would keep her informed of my progress. I finally asked her if she was satisfied with my planned actions and if there was anything else I could do to help her.

TOP TIPS FOR PASSING THE ROLE-PLAY EXERCISES

- Read all of the information thoroughly during the preparation phase. Take notes that are concise and relevant. For example:

  1. What is the centre's policy on drinking alcohol?
  2. What is the centre's policy on customer service?
  3. What is the centre's policy on fairness and equality?

- Once you have read all of the information and compiled your notes, prepare yourself for the activity phase.

- Remember to stay calm, be polite and courteous at all times and not to become defensive or angry.

- Ask probing questions in order to establish the facts.

- Tell the person/people making the complaint what the centre's policy is regarding the issue.

- Reassure them if necessary and tell them what your plan of action is in order to resolve the issue.

- Tell them that you will keep them informed of all progress.

- Ask them if they are satisfied with your actions so far and if there is anything else you can do to help.

THE INTERVIEW

Once the role-play stage of the assessment was complete, we were given a 20-minute break in which to prepare for the interview. Once again the recruitment centre staff provided us with a very good brief detailing exactly what would happen during the interview.

The interview panel will comprise of one or two people. The interviewers will be dressed in civilian clothes and will be either serving or retired Police Officers or qualified assessors who are not part of the Police Force.

The interview will comprise of 4 competency-based questions, therefore it is important that you know what the core competencies are. The 20 minutes spent in my car reading the competencies prior to the assessment certainly paid off during the interview! The best piece of advice I could give you prior to the interview is to try to come up with a number of different scenarios that you have experienced, either at work or in your social/personal life, that are based around the core competencies.

During my interview, which lasted 20 minutes, I was asked the following questions:

- Give a scenario where you have had to work as part of a team in order to achieve something.

- Give a scenario when you have had to be considerate to someone else's feelings.

- Give a scenario when you have had to show resilience and stick by what you believed.

- Give a scenario where you have had to help someone to improve his/her skills.

The above four questions are not guaranteed to be the exact ones that you will be asked at your assessment, but they will give you some indication as to what is required.

The interviewer may also ask you probing questions following your responses, in order to get the required information from you.

TOP TIPS FOR PASSING THE INTERVIEW

- Think of a scenario for each of the core competencies being assessed. Remember – this can be either from your work life, your personal life or your social life.

- Be polite, courteous, smile and be confident about your own abilities.

- Sit up straight in the chair and make 'non-confrontational' eye contact with the interviewer.

Once the interview was over we were then taken back to the briefing room.

Before leaving the assessment centre, some four hours after arriving, we were informed that we would receive our results within 2 weeks.

DISCLAIMER

The information provided in this section of the guide is for research purposes only. The reader should not rely on the information to be an exact reflection of what they will go through at the PCSO assessment centre. How2become Ltd is not responsible for anyone failing any part of the PCSO selection process as a result of the information contained within this guide.

CHAPTER 11

PCSO FITNESS TEST

INTRODUCTION

The majority of Police Forces do not require PCSO applicants to undertake a form of fitness assessment. However, there are some out there that do, and this section is designed for those people who are required to undertake one.

The type of fitness assessment still in use does vary from the multi-stage fitness test (bleep test), strength tests and even the Chester Step test. I will cover each of these areas in detail.

THE ENDURANCE TEST

The Endurance Test, also known as the Multi-Stage Fitness Test, Bleep or 'Shuttle Run' Test, is often used by sports coaches and trainers to estimate an athlete's VO2 Max (maximum oxygen uptake). Apart from the Police, the test is also used by the Armed Forces, Emergency Services and Prison Service as part of their selection process, but it is also a great way to improve and monitor your own fitness level.

Description

The Bleep test involves running continuously between two points that are 15m apart. These 'shuttle runs' are done in time to pre-recorded 'bleep' sounds on an audio CD or cassette. The time between the recorded 'bleeps' decreases after each minute and, therefore, the test becomes progressively harder with each level completed.

The full test consists of approximately 23 levels, but the actual Police Endurance Test only requires you to achieve 4 shuttles at level 5 to pass. Each level lasts approximately 60 seconds. A level is basically a series of 15 metre 'shuttle runs'. The starting speed is normally 8.5 km/hr, which then increases by 0.5km/hr with each new level.

THE DYNAMIC STRENGTH TEST

This test mimics a seated bench press action and a seated rowing action.

You will be asked to perform 5 repetitions on both the push and pull aspects. The machine works out the average of your 5 repetitions and gives you a score. You must Push 34 kg and Pull 35 kg to pass.

One of the most effective ways to prepare for this type of test is both by rowing (using a rowing machine) and carrying out bench press exercises. The reason why we recommend rowing during your preparation is that, apart from increasing your physical strength, it will also help prepare you for the endurance test.

Within the 'How to get PCSO fit' section of your guide I have provided you with some useful tips and exercises.

IMPORTANT: Make sure you consult a medical practitioner prior to engaging in any strenuous physical exercise programme.

THE CHESTER STEP TEST

The Chester Step test is used by a number of Police Forces during the PCSO selection process.

The step test is a sub maximal test that requires you to step onto, and off a 30 cm/12" step at a rate set by a metronome disc, sufficient to elicit a heart rate of around 80% of your maximum heart rate at a moderate level of exertion. It is a multi-staged test so every 2 minutes there is an increase in the rate of the step. Exercise heart rates are then plotted on a graph and aerobic capacity and fitness rating may be calculated.

Equipment needed:
- 30cm/12" Step.
- Heart Rate Monitor.
- Chester Step Test CD
- CD player.

Procedure for the Test

If you are doing your step test as part of your medical examination or as part of the selection process, then this will generally be the procedure that you will go through:

- Your maximum heart rate will be calculated (220 - Age) and then 80% of your maximum heart rate. These values will be entered in the appropriate box on the Chester Step Test Record sheet and two horizontal lines will be drawn on the graph to represent these values.

- A heart rate monitor will be attached to you, and you will be told what will be required of you during the test, followed by a brief demonstration of the initial stepping rate (15 steps/min).

- When the CD is turned on you will be encouraged to commence stepping at the appropriate stepping rate, and will continue to step for the next 2 minutes.

- After the first 2 minutes of stepping (stage 1) your heart rate will be recorded during the last few seconds of stepping. (You may also be asked to indicate your rating of perceived exertion (RPE) from a chart numbered 6 to 20, low scores being very, very light exertion and high scores being very, very hard exertion).

- Providing your heart rate is below 80% of your maximum heart rate and the RPE is below 14, you'll be asked to continue stepping at the slightly faster rate in stage 2 (20 steps/min).

- After another 2 minutes of stepping your heart rate will be recorded during the last few seconds of stage 2, and again you may be asked to indicate your RPE from the chart provided.

- Providing your heart rate is still below 80% of your maximum heart rate and the RPE is below 14, you'll be asked to continue stepping at the slightly faster rate in stage 3 (25 steps/min).

- The test will continue until either you report an RPE greater than 14 and/or an exercise heart rate greater than 80% of your maximum heart rate (stage 4 = 30 steps/min, stage 5 = 35 steps/min).

Your results will then be plotted and a decision will be made by the Occupational Doctor as to whether or not you pass the criteria for the step test.

CHAPTER 12

USEFUL CONTACT DETAILS

Within this section I have provided you with Police Contact information including telephone numbers and website addresses (Internet connection required). Contact the particular Police Force that you are interested in applying to join and see when they are recruiting.

You can also visit the Police National Recruitment website www.policecouldyou.co.uk for more details on PCSO recruitment.

If your particular force is not recruiting at the present time then it is worthwhile calling them to find out when they anticipate recruiting next. You can use this time wisely to help you to prepare for the pending recruitment drive. This will also give you some indication as to whether you wish to apply for a Police Force out of your home county area and then apply to transfer to your home one at a later date.

CONTACT DETAILS – NORTH EAST REGION

CLEVELAND POLICE
Telephone: 01642 301 479
www.cleveland.police.uk

DURHAM POLICE
Telephone: 0191 3752125
www.durham.police.uk

HUMBERSIDE POLICE
Telephone: 01482 220 096
www.humberside.police.uk

NORTHUMBRIA POLICE
Telephone: 01661 868 816
www.northumbria.police.uk

NORTH YORKSHIRE POLICE
Telephone: 01609 789 079
www.northyorkshire.police.uk

WEST YORKSHIRE POLICE
Telephone: 01924 292 069
www.westyorkshire.police.uk

SOUTH YORKSHIRE POLICE
Telephone: 0114 282 1234
www.southyorkshire.police.uk

CONTACT DETAILS – NORTH WEST REGION

CHESHIRE POLICE
Telephone: 01244 614 021
www.cheshire.police.uk

CUMBRIA POLICE
Telephone: 01768 217 092
www.cumbria.police.uk

GREATER MANCHESTER POLICE
Telephone: 0161 856 2333
www.gmp.police.uk

LANCASHIRE POLICE
PO Box 77 Hutton
Nr. Preston
Lancashire
PR4 5SB
www.lancashire.police.uk

MERSEYSIDE POLICE
Telephone: 0151 777 8238
www.merseyside.police.uk

CONTACT DETAILS – MIDLANDS REGION

WARWICKSHIRE POLICE
Telephone: 01926 415052
www.warwickshire.police.uk

WEST MERCIA POLICE
Telephone: 01905 723 000
www.westmercia.police.uk

WEST MIDLANDS POLICE
Telephone: 0121 626 5824
www.west-midlands.police.uk

LEICESTERSHIRE POLICE
Telephone: 0116 222 2222 ext. 2657
www.leics.police.uk

NORTHANTS POLICE
Telephone: 01604 703 091
www.northants.police.uk

STAFFORDSHIRE POLICE
Telephone: 01785 235353
www.staffordshire.police.uk

CONTACT DETAILS – WALES POLICE

DYFED POWYS POLICE
Telephone: 01267 222020
www.dyfed-powys.police.uk

GWENT POLICE
Telephone: (01495) 745407/745409
www.gwent.police.uk

NORTH WALES POLICE
Telephone: 01492 510019
www.north-wales.police.uk

SOUTH WALES POLICE
Telephone: 01656 869225
www.south-wales.police.uk

CONTACT DETAILS – SOUTH WEST REGION

AVON AND SOMERSET POLICE
Telephone: 01275 816142
www.avonandsomerset.police.uk

DEVON AND CORNWALL POLICE
Telephone: 01392 452500
www.devon-cornwall.police.uk

DORSET POLICE
Telephone: 01305 223 794
www.dorset.police.uk

GLOUCESTERSHIRE POLICE
Telephone: 0845 090 1234
www.gloucestershire.police.uk

WILTSHIRE POLICE
Telephone: 01380 722 341
www.wiltshire.police.uk

CONTACT DETAILS – SOUTH EAST REGION

METROPOLITAN POLICE
Telephone: 0845 727 2212 (8am-6pm)
www.metpolicecareers.co.uk

SURREY POLICE
Telephone: 01483 482266
www.surrey.police.uk

SUSSEX POLICE
Telephone: 01273 404 151
www.sussex.police.uk

THAMES VALLEY POLICE
Telephone: 01865 846 816
www.thamesvalley.police.uk

BRITISH TRANSPORT POLICE
Telephone: 020 7388 9121
www.btp.police.uk

CONTACT DETAILS – CENTRAL REGION

CAMBRIDGESHIRE POLICE
Telephone:0845 456 4564
www.cambridgeshire.police.uk

DERBYSHIRE POLICE
Telephone: 01773 572104
www.derbyshire.police.uk

LINCOLNSHIRE POLICE
Telephone: 01522 558235
www.lincolnshire.police.uk

NORFOLK POLICE
Telephone: 01953 423823
www.norfolk.police.uk

NOTTINGHAMSHIRE POLICE
Telephone: 0115 967 2424
www.nottinghamshire.police.uk

SUFFOLK POLICE
Telephone: 01473 613 640
www.suffolk.police.uk

CONTACT DETAILS – SCOTTISH POLICE

CENTRAL SCOTLAND POLICE
Telephone: 01786 456000
Fax: 01786 451177
Text-telephone: 01786 445533
www.centralscotland.police.uk

DUMFRIES AND GALLOWAY POLICE
Telephone: 01387 252112
Fax: 01387 260501
www.dumfriesandgalloway.police.uk

FIFE CONSTABULARY
Telephone: 01592 418888
www.fife.police.uk

GRAMPIAN POLICE
Telephone: 0845 6005700
www.grampian.police.uk

LOTHIAN AND BORDERS POLICE
Telephone: 0131 311 3131
www.lbp.police.uk

NORTHERN POLICE
Telephone: 01463 715 555
Fax: 01463 230 800
www.northern.police.uk

STRATHCLYDE POLICE
Telephone: 0141 532 2000
www.strathclyde.police.uk

TAYSIDE POLICE
Telephone: 01382 223200
Fax: 01382 200449
www.tayside.police.uk

CHAPTER 13

HOW TO GET
PCSO FIT

INTRODUCTION

Within this guide I have provided you with a number of useful exercises that will allow you to prepare for, and pass, the PCSO fitness test. As previously stated, the majority of Police Forces will not require you to undertake a fitness test. However, it will still be your responsibility to ensure that you are fit enough to perform your role effectively. This guide will provide with some fantastic exercises that will go a long way to keeping you at peak performance.

The fitness test is not difficult to pass, providing you put in the time and effort to reach a good all-round level of fitness. PCSOs need to have a good all-round aerobic fitness and also a good level of strength and stamina. The exercises contained within this guide will help you to achieve exactly that. Do not spend hours in the gym lifting heavy weights as the job does not require that level of strength, but rather aim for a varied and diverse fitness programme that covers exercises such as swimming, rowing, jogging, brisk walking and light weight work.

In addition to getting fit, keep an eye on your diet and try to eat healthy foods whilst drinking plenty of water. It will all go a long way to helping you improve your general well-being and concentration levels whilst you prepare for the selection process.

PLANNING YOUR WORKOUTS AND PREPARING FOR THE PCSO FITNESS TESTS

Most people who embark on a fitness regime in January have given it up by February. The reason why most people give up their fitness regime so soon is mainly due to a lack of proper preparation. You will recall that throughout the duration of this guide the word preparation has been integral, and the same word applies when preparing for the fitness tests. Preparation is key to your success and it is essential that you plan your workouts effectively.

To begin with, try to think about the role of a PCSO and what it entails. You will have to run pretty fast on some occasions and you will also need a level of strength for certain operational tasks. In the build-up to the physical tests I advise that you concentrate on specific exercises that will allow you to pass the tests with ease. Read on for some great ways to pass the PCSO fitness tests and stay fit all year round.

Get an assessment before you start training

The first step is to get a fitness test at the gym, weigh yourself and run your fastest mile. Once you have done all three of these you should write down your results and keep them hidden away somewhere safe. After a month of following your new fitness regime, do all three tests again and check your results against the previous month's. This is a great way to monitor your performance and progress and it will also keep you motivated and focused on your goals.

Keep a check on what you eat and drink

Make sure you write down everything you eat and drink for a whole week. You must include tea, water, milk, biscuits and anything and everything that you digest. You will soon begin to realise how much you are eating and you will notice areas in which you can make some changes. For example, if you are taking sugar with your tea then why not try reducing it or giving it up altogether. If you do then you will soon notice the difference.

It is important that you start to look for opportunities to improve your fitness and well-being right from the offset.

These areas are what I call 'easy wins'.

Exercises that will help you to pass the fitness tests

It is my strong belief that you do not have to attend a gym in order to prepare for the PCSO fitness tests. If I was applying to become a police community support officer today then I would embark on a fitness programme that included brisk walking, running, rowing, press-ups, sit-ups, squats and lunges. In order to improve my upper body strength I would also go swimming.

Walking is one of the best exercises you can do as part of your preparation for the PCSO fitness tests. Whilst it shouldn't be the only form of exercise you carry out, it will go a long way to improving your focus and general well-being. Now when I say 'walking' I don't mean a gentle stroll, I mean 'brisk' walking. Try walking at a fast pace for 30 minutes every day for a 7-day period. Then see how you feel at the end of the 7 days. I guarantee you'll begin to feel a lot healthier and fitter. Brisk walking is also a fantastic way to lose weight if you think you need to. In addition to helping you to lose weight it will also keep your concentration and motivational levels up.

There are some more great exercises contained within this guide and most of them can be carried out without the need to attend a gym.

One step at a time

Only you will know how fit you are. I advise that you first of all write down the areas that you believe or feel you need to improve on. For example, if you feel that you need to work on your upper body strength then pick out exercises from this guide that will work on that area for you. I also advise that you obtain a copy of the multi-stage fitness test and practise it. Make sure you can easily pass the required standard.

The key to making improvements is to do it gradually, and at one step at a time. Try to set yourself small goals. If you think you need to lose two stone in weight then focus on losing a few pounds at a time. For example, during the first month aim to lose 6 pounds only. Once you have achieved this then again aim to lose 6 pounds over the next month, and so on and so forth. The more realistic your goal, the more likely you are to achieve it. One of the biggest problems people encounter when starting a fitness regime is that they become bored quickly. This then leads to a lack of motivation and desire, and soon the fitness programme stops.

Change your exercise routine often. Instead of walking try jogging. Instead of jogging try cycling with the odd day of swimming. Keep your workouts varied and interesting to ensure that you stay focused and motivated.

STRETCHING

How many people stretch before carrying out any form of exercise? Very few people, is the correct answer! Not only is it irresponsible but it is also placing you at high risk from injury. Before we commence with the exercises we will take a look at a few warm-up stretches. Make sure you stretch fully before carrying out any exercises. You want your career as a PCSO to be a long one and that means looking after yourself, including stretching! It is also very important to check with your GP that you are medically fit to carry out any form of physical exercise.

The warm-up calf stretch

To perform this stretch effectively you should first of all start off by facing a wall whilst standing upright. Your right foot should be close to the wall and your right knee bent. Now place your hands flat against the wall and at a height that is level with your shoulders. Stretch your left leg far out behind you, without lifting your toes and heel off the floor, and lean towards the wall.

Once you have performed this stretch for 25 seconds, switch legs and carry out the same procedure for the right leg. As with all exercises contained within this guide, stop if you feel any pain or discomfort.

Stretching the shoulder muscles

To begin with, stand with your feet slightly apart and with your knees only slightly bent. Now hold your arms right out in front of you, with your palms facing away from you and with your fingers pointing skywards. Now place your right palm on the back of your left hand and use it to push the left hand further away from you. If you are performing this exercise correctly then you will feel the muscles in your shoulder stretching. Hold for 10 seconds before switching sides.

Stretching the quad muscles (front of the thigh)

Before you carry out any form of brisk walking or running, it is imperative that you stretch your leg muscles. During the fitness tests, and especially prior to the multi-stage fitness test, the instructors should take you through a series of warm-up exercises, which will include stretching the quad muscles. To begin with, stand with your right hand pressed against the back of a wall or firm surface. Bend your left knee and bring your left heel up to your bottom whilst grasping your foot with your left hand. Your back should be straight and your shoulders, hips and knees should all be in line at all times during the exercise. Hold for 25 seconds before switching legs.

Stretching the hamstring muscles (back of the thigh)

To perform this exercise correctly, stand up straight and place your right foot onto a table or other firm surface so that your leg is almost parallel to the floor. Keep your left leg straight and your foot at a right angle to your leg. Start to slowly move your hands down your right leg towards your ankle until you feel tension on the underside of your thigh. When you feel this tension you know that you are starting to stretch the hamstring muscles. Hold for 25 seconds before switching legs.

We have only covered a small number of stretching exercises within this section; however, it is crucial that you stretch out fully in all areas before carrying out any of the following exercises. Remember to obtain professional advice before carrying out any type of exercise.

RUNNING

As I have already mentioned, one of the best ways to prepare for the PCSO fitness tests is to embark on a structured running programme. You do not need to run at a fast pace or even run for long distances, in order to gain massively from this type of exercise.

Before I joined the Fire Service I spent a few years in the Royal Navy. I applied to join the Navy when I was 16 and I made it through the selection process with ease until I reached the medical. During the medical the doctor told me that I was overweight and that I had to lose a stone before they would accept me. To be honest, I was heartbroken. I couldn't believe it; especially after all the hard work I had put in preparing for the tests and the interview! Anyway, as soon as I arrived back home from the medical I started out on a structured running programme that would see me lose the stone in weight within only 4 weeks! The following running programme is very similar to the one I used all those years ago and it will serve you well when preparing for the fitness tests.

Before I provide you with the running programme, however, take a read of the following important running tips.

Tips for running

- As with any exercise, you should consult a doctor before taking part to make sure that you are medically fit.

- It is certainly worth investing in a pair of comfortable running shoes that serve the purpose for your intended training programme. Your local sports shop will be able to advise you on the types that are best for you. You don't have to spend a fortune to buy a good pair of running shoes.

- It is a good idea to invest in a 'high visibility' jacket or coat so that you can be seen by fast moving traffic if you intend to run on or near the road.

- Make sure you carry out at least 5 whole minutes of stretching exercises not only before but also after your running programme. This can help to prevent injury.

- Whilst you shouldn't run on a full stomach, it is also not good to run on an empty one either. A great food to eat approximately 30 minutes before a run is a banana. This is great for giving you energy.

- Drink plenty of water throughout the day. Try to drink at least 1.5 litres each day in total. This will keep you hydrated and help to prevent muscle cramp.

- Don't overdo it. If you feel any pain or discomfort then stop and seek medical advice.

RUNNING PROGRAMME WEEK 1

DAY 1
• Run a total of 3 miles only at a steady pace.

If you cannot manage 3 miles then try the following:

• Walk at a brisk pace for half a mile or approximately 10 minutes.

Then
• Run for 1 mile or 8 minutes.

Then
• Walk for another half a mile or approximately 10 minutes.

Then
• Run for 1.5 miles or 12 minutes.

Walking at a brisk pace is probably the most effective way to lose weight if you need to. It is possible to burn the same amount of calories if you walk the same distance as if you were running.

When walking at a 'brisk' pace it is recommended that you walk as fast as is comfortably possible without breaking into a run or slow jog.

DAY 2
• Walk for 2 miles or approximately 20 minutes at a brisk pace.

Then
• Run for 2 miles or 14 minutes.

DAY 3
• Repeat DAY ONE.

DAY 4

- Walk at a brisk pace for 0.5 miles or approximately 7 minutes.

Then
- Run for 3 miles or 20 minutes.

DAY 5
- Repeat DAY ONE.

DAY 6 AND DAY 7
- Rest days. No exercise.

RUNNING PROGRAMME WEEK 2

DAY 1
- Run for 4 miles or 25 minutes.

DAY 2
- Run a total of 3 miles at a steady pace.

If you cannot manage 3 miles then try the following:

- Walk at a brisk pace for half a mile or approximately 10 minutes.

Then
- Run for 1 mile or 8 minutes.

Then
- Walk for another half a mile or approximately 10 minutes.

Then
- Run for 1.5 miles or 12 minutes.

DAY 3
- Rest day. No exercise.

DAY 4

• Run for 5 miles or 35 to 40 minutes.

DAY 5

• Run for 3 miles or 20 minutes.

Then

• Walk at a brisk pace for 2 miles or approximately 20 minutes.

DAY 6

• Run for 5 miles or 35 to 45 minutes.

DAY 7

• Rest day. No exercise.

Once you have completed the second week running programme, use the third week to perform different types of exercises, such as cycling and swimming. During week 4 you can then commence the 2-week running programme again. You'll be amazed at how much easier it is the second time around!

When preparing for the selection process, use your exercise time as a break from your studies. For example, if you have been working on the application form for a couple of hours, why not take a break and go running? When you return from your run you can then concentrate on your studies feeling refreshed.

Now that I've provided you with a structured running programme to follow, there really are no excuses. So, get out there and start running! I'll now provide you with a number of key targeted exercises that will allow you to prepare effectively for the PCSO fitness tests.

EXERCISES THAT WILL IMPROVE YOUR ABILITY TO PASS THE PCSO FITNESS TESTS

Press-ups

Whilst running is a great way to improve your overall fitness, you will also need to carry out exercises that improve your upper body strength. These exercises will help you to pass the strength tests, which may form part of the assessment. The great thing about press-ups is that you don't have to attend a gym to perform them. However, you must ensure that you can do them correctly as injury can occur. You only need to spend just 5 minutes every day on press-ups, possibly after you go running or even before if you prefer. If you are not used to doing press-ups then start slowly and aim to carry out at least 10.

Even if you struggle to do just 10, you will soon find that after a few days' practice at these you will be up to 20+.

Step 1 - To begin with, lie on a mat or even surface. Your hands should be shoulder width apart and your arms fully extended.

Step 2 - Gradually lower your body until the elbows reach 90°. Do not rush the movement as you may cause injury.

Step 3 - Once your elbows reach 90° slowly return to the starting position with your arms fully extended.

The press-up action should be a continuous movement with no rest. However, it is important that the exercise is as smooth as possible and there should be no jolting or sudden movements. Try to complete as many press-ups as possible and always keep a record of how many you do. This will keep you focused and also maintain your motivation levels.

Did you know that the world record for non-stop press-ups is currently 10,507 set in 1980!

WARNING – Ensure you take advice from a competent fitness trainer in relation to the correct execution of press-up exercises and other exercises contained within this guide.

Sit-ups

Sit-ups are great for building the core stomach muscles. At the commencement of the exercise lie flat on your back with your knees bent at a 45° angle and with your feet together. Your hands can either be crossed on your chest, by your sides, or cupped behind your ears.

Without moving your lower body, curl your upper torso upwards and in towards your knees, until your shoulder blades are as high off the ground as possible. As you reach the highest point, tighten your abdominal muscles for a brief second. This will allow you to get the most out of the exercise. Now slowly start to lower yourself back to the starting position. You should be aiming to work up to at least 50 effective sit-ups every day. You will be amazed at how quickly this can be achieved and you will begin to notice your stomach muscles developing.

Whilst sit-ups do not form part of fitness tests, they are still a great way of improving your all-round fitness and therefore should not be neglected.

Pull-ups

Pull-ups are another great way for building the core upper body muscle groups. The unfortunate thing about this type of exercise is you will probably need to attend a gym in order to carry them out. Having said that, there are a number of different types of 'pull-up bars' available to buy on the market that can easily and safely be fitted to a doorway at home. If you choose to purchase one of these items make sure that it conforms to the relevant safety standards first.

Lateral pull-ups are very effective at increasing upper body strength. If you have access to a gymnasium then these can be practised on a 'lateral pull-up' machine. It is advised that you consult a member of staff at your gym to ask about these exercises.

Pull-ups should be performed by firmly grasping a sturdy and solid bar. Before you grasp the bar make sure it is safe. Your hands should be roughly shoulder-width apart. Straighten your arms so that your body hangs loose. You will feel your lateral muscles and biceps stretching as you hang in the air. This is the starting position for the lateral pull-up exercise.

Next, pull yourself upwards to the point where your chest is almost touching the bar and your chin is actually over the bar. Whilst pulling upwards, focus on keeping your body straight without any arching or swinging as this can result in injury. Once your chin is over the bar, you can lower yourself back down to the initial starting position. Repeat the exercise 10 times.

Squats (these work the legs and bottom)
Squats are a great exercise for working the leg muscles. They are the perfect exercise in your preparation for the PCSO fitness tests.

At the commencement of the exercise, stand up straight with your arms at your sides. Concentrate on keeping your feet shoulder-width apart and your head up. Do not look downwards at any point during the exercise.

Now start to very slowly bend your knees while pushing your rear out as though you are about to sit down on a chair. Keep lowering yourself down until your thighs reach past the 90° point. Make sure your weight is on your heels so that your knees do not extend over your toes. At this point you may wish to tighten your thighs and buttocks to intensify the exercise.

As you come back up to a standing position, push down through your heels, which will allow you to maintain your balance. Repeat the exercise 15 to 20 times.

Lunges (these work the thighs and bottom)

You will have noticed throughout this section of the guide that I have been providing you with simple, yet highly effective exercises that can be carried out at home. The lunge exercise is another great addition to the range of exercises that require no attendance at the gym.

To begin with, stand with your back straight and your feet together (you may hold light hand weights if you wish to add some intensity to the exercise).

Next, take a big step forward, making sure you inhale as go and landing with the heel first. Bend the front knee no more than 90 degrees so as to avoid injury. Keep your back straight and lower the back knee as close to the floor as possible. Your front knee should be lined up over your ankle and your back thigh should be in line with your back.

To complete the exercise, exhale and push down against your front heel, squeezing your buttocks tight as you rise back to the starting position.

Try to repeat the exercise 15 to 20 times before switching sides.

Lateral raises (these work the shoulder muscles)

Whilst PCSOs are not usually required to lift heavy items of equipment during their day-to-day work, they still need to have a good level of upper body strength. Lateral raises will allow you to improve your upper body strength in a safe and effective manner.

Take a dumbbell in each hand and hold them by the sides of your body with your palms facing inwards.

Stand or sit with your feet shoulder-width apart, knees slightly bent. Do not lean backwards as you could cause injury to your back. Raise your arms up and out to the sides until they are parallel to the ground, then lower them back down carefully. Repeat the exercise 15 to 20 times.

ALTERNATIVE EXERCISES

Swimming

Apart from press-ups, lateral raises and the other exercises I have provided you with, another fantastic way to improve your upper body and overall fitness is to go swimming. If you have access to a swimming pool, and you can swim, then this is a brilliant way to improve your fitness.

If you are not a great swimmer you can start off with short distances and gradually build up your swimming strength and stamina. Breaststroke is sufficient for building good upper body strength providing you put the effort into swimming an effective number of lengths. You may wish to alternate your running programme with the odd day of swimming. If you can swim 10 lengths of a 25-metre pool initially then this is a good base to start from. You will soon find that you can increase this number easily providing that you carry on swimming every week. Try running to your local swimming pool, if it is not too far away, swimming 20 lengths of breaststroke, and then running back home.

This is a great way to combine your fitness activity and prevent yourself from becoming bored of your training programme.

Rowing

If there is one exercise that will allow you to work every single muscle group in the body then it is rowing. This is the perfect exercise for preparing to pass the fitness tests. It will increase your aerobic fitness and it will also improve your lower and upper body strength. As with any exercise of this nature there is a risk of injury. It is crucial that you use the correct technique when rowing on a purpose-built machine. By applying the correct technique you will be far more efficient and you will also see faster results.

Whilst exercising on the rowing machine, make sure you keep your back straight and concentrate on using your legs and buttocks. Never extend so far that you lock out your knees. Try to be smooth throughout the entire exercise. To obtain a suitable indoor rowing training programme that is relevant to your current fitness levels please visit www. concept2.co.uk.

The multi-stage fitness test or bleep test

This part of the selection process (if applicable) requires you to demonstrate a specific level of fitness. In simple terms the bleep test requires you to run backwards and forwards (shuttles) between 2 fixed points a set distance apart. The test is progressive in that as the levels increase so does the difficulty.

A tape will be played that contains a series of 'bleeps' set out at different intervals. The distance between the 'bleeps' at level 1 will be far greater than the 'bleeps' at level 10. Each time the 'bleeps' increase, the tape will let you know that you are progressing to the next level. During the test you will be required to keep up with 'bleeps' and not fall behind them or run ahead of them. Level 1 starts off at around walking pace and gradually increases as each stage progresses.

The best way to practise for this stage of the test is to practise the actual test itself. However, the next best alternative is to go running for at least 3 miles, at least 3 times a week. Each time you go out running you should try to push yourself a little bit harder and further.

By running 3 times a week you will give your body the rest it needs in between each run so it is probably best to run on alternate days.

TIPS FOR STAYING WITH YOUR WORKOUT

The hardest part of your training programme will be sticking with it. In this final section of your fitness guide I will provide some useful golden rules that will enable you to maintain your motivational levels in the build-up to the PCSO tests. In order to stay with your workout for longer, try following these simple rules:

Golden rule number one - Work out often

Aim to train three to five times each and every week.

Each training session should last between 20 minutes to a maximum of an hour. The quality of training is important so don't go for heavy weights but instead go for a lighter weight with a better technique. On days when you are feeling energetic, take advantage of this opportunity and do more!

Within this guide I have deliberately provided you with a number of 'simple-to-perform' exercises that are targeted at the core muscle groups required to perform the role of a PCSO. In between your study sessions try carrying out these exercises at home or get yourself out on the road running or cycling. Use your study 'down-time' effectively and wisely.

Golden rule number two - Mix up your exercises

Your exercise programme should include some elements of cardiovascular (aerobics, running, brisk walking and cycling), resistance training (weights or own body exercises such as press-ups and sit-ups) and, finally, flexibility (stretching). Make sure that you always warm up and warm down.

If you are a member of a gym then consider taking up a class such as Pilates. This form of exercise class will teach you how to build core training into your exercise principles, and show you how to hit your abdominals in ways that are not possible with conventional sit-ups. If you are a member of a gym then a fantastic 'all-round' exercise that I strongly recommend is rowing. Rowing will hit every major muscle group in your body and it is also perfect for improving your stamina levels and cardiovascular fitness.

Golden rule number three - Eat a healthy and balanced diet

It is vitally important that you eat the right fuel to give you the energy to train to your full potential. Don't fill your body with rubbish and then expect to train well. Think about what you are eating and drinking, including the quantities, and keep a record of what you are digesting. You will become stronger and fitter more quickly if you eat little amounts of nutritious foods at short intervals.

Golden rule number four - Get help

Try working with a personal trainer. They will ensure that you work hard and will help you to achieve your goals. If you cannot afford a personal trainer then try training with someone else. The mere fact that they are there at your side will add an element of competition to your training sessions!

A consultation with a professional nutritionist will also help you improve your eating habits and establish your individual food needs.

Golden rule number five - Fitness is for life
One of my old managers in the Fire Service had a saying – "Fitness Wins!" Two simple words that meant an awful lot! Improving your fitness and eating healthily are not short-term projects. They are things that should come naturally to you.

Make fitness a permanent part of your life by following these tips, and you'll lead a better and more fulfilling life!

Good luck and work hard to improve your weak areas.

CHAPTER 14

FREQUENTLY
ASKED QUESTIONS

What is a Police Community Support Officer (PCSO)?

PCSOs are members of support staff employed, directed and managed by the Police. They work alongside police officers to provide a visible and accessible uniformed presence to improve the quality of life in the community and offer greater public reassurance.

Are PCSOs used as a replacement for regular police officers?

No, PCSOs are used in addition to existing police officers.

Are PCSOs the same as Special Constables?

No, PCSOs have a unique role designed purely to tackle antisocial behaviour and quality of life issues. While Special Constables are unpaid volunteers with similar powers to that of regular full-time police officers, PCSOs are paid Support Staff employees with their own unique powers.

Why are Police Forces employing PCSOs?

Public demand for visible patrols has never been greater. The Police have taken advantage of new opportunities arising from Government reforms of policing to increase their capacity to meet this demand and deliver the service that the community expect and deserve.

Where do PCSOs work?

They work within the county area as defined by the relevant Police Force.

If I am unsuccessful at any stage of the recruitment process, when can I re-apply?

If you are unsuccessful at any stage of the process, you will not have to wait any length of time before you can re-apply. However, Police Forces recruit at certain times of the year and you can only re-apply if they are recruiting.

Do I have to be tall to be a PCSO?
No, there are no height restrictions in place.

How long is my probationary period?
The probationary period for PCSOs is 12 months.

How old do I have to be to apply to become a PCSO?
At present, you can apply to become a PCSO at the age of 18.

Can I apply with criminal convictions?
You may be eligible to join with minor convictions or cautions, but this depends on how old you were at the time and what the conviction or caution was for. There are certain types of offences that will lead to instant rejection, such as murder, manslaughter, death by reckless driving, rape, kidnapping, firearms offences, gross indecency, hostage taking, hijacking or torture. Please check with your local Police Force to verify this information.

Do I have to be a British Citizen?
To be eligible for appointment you must be a British Citizen, an EC or EEA national, a Commonwealth Citizen or a Foreign National with no restrictions on your stay in the UK. You must also have lived in the UK for a minimum of 3 years prior to your application.

If I am female, or a member of a minority group, will my application be discriminated against?
No, all Police Forces welcome and encourage applications from females and ethnic minority groups. The principles of fair and open competition apply and appointments will be made on merit.

Can I apply if I have tattoos?

Yes, as long as your tattoo will not cause offence to members of the public or your colleagues.

What qualifications do I need to become a PCSO?

There are no formal educational requirements to become a PCSO, but applicants must undergo a written test at the Selection Centre. Therefore, a reasonable standard of English is required.

How can PCSOs be effective without full police powers?

PCSOs are not police officers. Their main role is to deal with quality of life issues that do not always require the presence of a police officer. All PCSOs will be given full training to enable them to take appropriate action in the event of difficult circumstances. They will be supervised by police officers and will carry radios to enable them to call for assistance, should it be required.

Why don't the Police just employ more police constables?

The Police do continue to employ as many police officers as Government funding allows. However, they also need to provide a more visible and accessible uniformed foot patrol and tackle quality of life issues. These tasks do not always require the powers or experience of police officers, but often take them away from more appropriate duties.

How can you tell a PCSO from a police officer?

PCSOs have their own style of uniform, which makes it easier to tell the difference between them and regular police officers. PCSOs have blue bands around their hats, blue ties, and blue epaulettes on their shoulders. On the back of their coat or jacket it says POLICE COMMUNITY SUPPORT OFFICER. All PCSOs also carry personal identification with them.

What equipment do PCSOs carry?

PCSOs will wear protective vests, but will not carry other personal protection equipment such as CS spray or batons. They will all have a personal radio that provides immediate access to police communications and support.

Do PCSOs work shifts?

Yes.

Are there opportunities to work part-time and flexible hours as a PCSO?

Yes, part-time and flexible hours are usually considered.

What powers do PCSOs have?

All PCSOs have the following powers:

* Issuing fixed penalty notices (e.g. for riding on footpaths, dog fouling and litter).

* Confiscating alcohol and tobacco.

* Entering property to save life or prevent damage.

* Demanding the name and address of a person acting in an antisocial manner.

* Removing abandoned vehicles.

* Seizing vehicles being used to cause alarm or distress.

A FEW FINAL WORDS

You have now reached the end of the guide and no doubt you will be ready to start preparing for the PCSO selection process. Just before you go off and start on your preparation, consider the following.

The majority of candidates who pass the selection process have a number of common attributes. These are as follows:

1. They believe in themselves.
The first factor is self-belief. Regardless of what anyone tells you, you can become a PCSO. Just like any job of this nature, you have to be prepared to work hard in order to be successful. Make sure you have the self-belief to pass the selection process and fill your mind with positive thoughts.

2. They prepare fully.
The second factor is preparation. Those people who achieve in life prepare fully for every eventuality and that is what you must do when you apply to become a police community support officer. Work very hard and especially concentrate on your weak areas.

3. They persevere.
Perseverance is a fantastic word. Everybody comes across obstacles or setbacks in their life, but it is what you do about those setbacks that is important. If you fail at something, then ask yourself 'why' you have failed. This will allow you to improve for next time and if you keep improving and trying, success will eventually follow. Apply this same method of thinking when you apply to become a police community support officer.

4. They are self-motivated.

How much do you want this job? Do you want it, or do you really want it?

When you apply to join the police as a PCSO you should want it more than anything in the world. Your levels of self-motivation will shine through on your application and during your interview. For the weeks and months leading up to the selection process, be motivated as best you can and always keep your fitness levels up as this will serve to increase your levels of motivation.

Work hard, stay focused and be what you want...

Richard McMunn

how2become

**Visit www.how2become.com to find more titles
and courses that will help you to pass the
PCSO selection process, including:**

- How to pass the PCSO Role-Play DVD.

- How to pass the PCSO Interview DVD.

- 1-Day PCSO training course.

- Psychometric testing books and CDs.

www.how2become.com